Mind Ya Busi-ness:
Are You Okay?

Mind Ya Busi-ness:
Are You Okay?

LATONYA BYNUM, CEO, MPH, CHES ®

© 2020 by LaTonya Bynum, MPH, CHES

All rights reserved. No portion of this book may be reproduced in any form without permission from the publisher, except as permitted by U.S. copyright law.

For permissions contact:

info@latonyabynum.com

Cover and interior design: Sophisticated Press LLC

ISBN: 978-0-578-72177-4

Printed in the United States of America

This book is dedicated to the memory of three of the best:

Nettie Fikes Steward, The Granny

Elaunda Simmons Pirtle, The Cousin

D'Andre Eric Banks, The High School Classmate

TABLE OF CONTENTS

Acknowledgements

1. You Know Her 1
2. Poor In Spirit 12
3. Sugar Daddy 21
4. In Hell vs. Inhale Stress 25
5. I Am Not Stopping 34
6. Are You Okay? 38
7. Mindset Strong 45
8. Straight A & B People 53
9. Obesity Suicide 60
10. Truth Triggers 69
11. She Weird 74
12. Wake Up 81
13. Glow Up 88
14. Dear Me 98
15. Survival of the Fittest 110
16. Success Her Way 120
17. The Wise One 132
18. Broken Curses 140
19. Creative Genius 148
20. No Excuses 154

About The Author 165

About URA Resource Center, LLC 167

Acknowledgements

Saying you are not okay is the start of "Minding Ya Business"! In 2017, I confessed "I am not happy" and set out to start minding my own business. The stories, thoughts and challenges I faced with mastering the process are detailed in this book as practical techniques that when mastered are going to catapult your life, career and business 10 years ahead of schedule.

First giving honor to the most high for giving me this assignment to share my journey forward in my own words, true, raw, real and uncut.

Secondly, I would like to thank all my haters who were my foot stool in helping me to get to where I am today. You have been and will always continue to be one of my greatest motivators. Thank you!

Thanks to all my family (Mom – Brenda Kay, Dad – James Larry and 3 Kids – Calvin Jr., Khalia and Calaysia who have continued supporting me throughout this 2nd book project), small circle of friends (Rachel, Nicholaus and Louise) who get me and those who have supported me along this journey. You are the real MVP and you know who you are.

Last but not least, many thank you's to all of the People Champs out there in the world especially the ones down south who are often overlooked, undervalued and misunderstood –

you are the epitome of why and how "Minding Ya Business" works in everyone's favor if they take time out to put the technique and life lessons into play.

1   You Know Her

Her dreams of reaching the unreachable began to come true. She had the dream for several years but the fear paralyzed her. Her anecdote for fear was swift and strategic action. The opportunity outweighed the risk... Her new name was "risk-taker".

She had what it takes to be an amazing woman. Her past was behind her. She had laid everything out on the table for all to see. Some were inspired, others sad, and most didn't care either way. Reality had set in that she now was considered a fearless woman. Armed with high emotional intelligence, valuable skills, and a network of powerful leaders - she had what was needed to be WONDERWOMAN

A cry for help was cast out in a sea of unhappiness. Most could not imagine the deep sadness that was within themselves. They were socially programmed for unhappiness. She cried out for answers and there were none. That day she learned something about herself and others. You see to heal the community of the depression and unhappiness she had to be honest about the root cause. The root cause was a simple childhood memory. To unblock her next level of potential she had to go back to that memory. Going back to that day and healing that pain helped her to move forward with her future. Her future was bright and now she could see the light. She moved quickly as she saw more light. That energy, inspiration, and healing led the way for herself and others to cast their net towards a new sea. They called her "Healer".

She had success but she lacked purpose. It was time to marry the two on Wednesday. As she prepared her mind, body and soul she finally understood true happiness comes from within. It is an eternal dying of self that allowed her to truly inspire. She had no regrets as she lived a life that truly reflected her vision of a woman of God, a mother, a wife, and a sister to many. Her sole purpose was not to accumulate assets but instead give assets and quality resources to those with very few to none. The success was now for a purpose. They called her "Resourceful" because she could analyze any situation then provide resources to meet the root cause of the problem. Astonishing all who were ten times smarter than she...she was WISE beyond her years!

The people we least expect to do and say things that we need the most are just beginning to show up and show out in a BIG way. Welcome them with open arms and simply tell them thanks then pay It FORWARD

My new song before bed...

One day work won't be work it'll be fun

That day that day will soon come

I pray I pray God show me the way

Until that day that day I'll accept hourly pay

She was a beautiful flower blooming daily...They attempted to pluck her but she kept blooming. Her roots were sown into strong foundation rich in nourishment. As she grew, she began to inspire other flowers to blossom. It was their season...

Through my lifelong personal research I have found that TEN percent (10%) of folks I know are easily inspired but the other 90% only move if you aggravate them - got to strike a nerve within them to get them to MOVE.

Once you strike a nerve within them then they get activated and fired up. Just need to give them a little direction after they are fired up and ready.

Lead them to where you found yourself!

Be patient with those who don't know!

Consider the time when you were lost!

Find joy in being a trusted guiding light!

Your reward will be to see their new way!

Deep down soul stirring joy is what I feel!

God is the source of my light!

Put that same energy and focus that it took to get that degree into getting your health on track. All that wisdom and potential in a temple that's decaying!

The physical follows the mental

I really had no one to share my good news with yesterday because I didn't want 39 questions about why I made the original decision in the first place. Ya'll know how you are...Tonya, I thought you were smart I would have never did that in the first place. Blah Blah Blah Blah - I don't want to hear any of it lol...

Hell I am human and being human doesn't mean I am perfect.

Today, I want to remind someone that there is another option to get out of your situation. Don't just pray about it...get off your ass, meditate on the outcome and not the problem (try meditating without the weed lol), research some options online, ask random questions to people you know, hell ask strangers what they think they might have clues too, and use your phone to make some calls once you made a final decision. Sit back and watch it work out from there!

Last but not least do something about it don't just sit there being hopeless and angry. You are wasting precious time focused on the wrong thing. LaTonya Bynum loves you and wants you to try your very best to make a come up. Thank me later.

All the motivating QUOTES, encouraging SERMONS, inspirational TEXTS, and empowering PHONE CALLS aren't effective if you haven't set GOALS.

The quotes, sermons, texts, phone calls are only effective when we have set goals that we TRULY believe in. With no goals, you are sad-mad, depressed, and no fun to be around because you lack a vision for your life.

This week, let's set GOALS so BIG that most people can only imagine it truly happening. By this Friday, you will have put in the necessary work. You believe in YOURSELF and your ability to make your DREAM come true!

Our goals must motivate, encourage, inspire, and empower us to get off our ASS and work using our mind, hands, and feet to accomplish our wildest dreams. Get Going!

No more feeling guilty about all that you have accomplished. You see, when they were sitting around complaining, watching countless hours of TV and hanging out being the life of the party you were minding your business perfecting your vision. They think you are an overnight success but to be honest you understood the importance of sacrifice and delayed gratification as a teenager. You had a head start because you made your mind up early that your vision was rare. Now they sad-mad, depressed, and no fun to be around because you got what they want. They can't have what you got until they put in the work like you have. They either inspired or jealous. Note the difference.

One day I am going to tell my story and a lot of y'all gone be shocked but be immediately healed.

This week I am getting some shit off my chest so I can truly be free from childhood molestation by a family member I still see everyday.

This is holding me back from an international platform of sharing my greatness with the world. No more shame, guilt, depression, anxiety, or relationships that hinder my full potential. The real LaTonya Bynum Story is untold. Some real Lifetime movie shit if you ask me.

The truth will heal the obesity, high blood pressure, ALL forms of CANCEROUS cells and heart disease epidemic leading to the shutdown of state health departments, clinics, and hospitals all over the world! It's not what YOU are eating. It is what is eating YOU!

The silent suffering epidemic is over FOREVER.

It is amazing what you can accomplish if and when you put yourself first. No harm intended but we don't have time for bull crap farts followed by complaining moans then groans. Take that somewhere else please sir and ma'am.

You can always tell when you want to be around someone or NOT!

The truth is so clear. As we grow and mature, there are certain people, family members, coworkers, associates and neighbors that we are going to have to CUT off. It is a fact that our lives are taking a new direction as we head into next year. We are beginning to see a clear path towards what it is going to take to go higher and SOAR like the eagle we know we are. There are some folks that we will and must decide to leave in this year. They don't add anything of value to our lives. They truly aren't doing any more this year than they have done in this year or in the past years that you have known them.

Out of pity and complacency, you keep them around because they help you feel so much better about your situation. You needed them and they needed you at one point in time - it was more of a power struggle of both of you becoming better than *your best. Their lives simply makes you want to keep going more in the direction you are going. They remind you constantly of who you used to be and you keep running from that person you used to be - you definitely NEVER want to go back to being that PERSON again.*

They look at you as if you are the wind beneath their wings. If you were to ever leave them or did not call them with encouragement, motivation, and inspiration then they wouldn't know what to do. Truth is you could use the same inspiration, motivation, and encouragement that you give out to them BUT they never give you what you need. You constantly are pouring and depleting your heart, soul, and mind into trying to resurrect them. All these years seem as if there has not been anything gained from your time, energy and money spent with them. You realize today that they have helped you in so many ways to be great listener, comforter, encourager, advisor, and all around great person for someone who can reciprocate at your level. Just know it was for a purpose that you spent your time with them. Nothing lost and nothing gained.

You see, today is a new day and a new chance to free yourself of them. They are not going to be any more than they want for themselves. In order for their life to get on track, it is an absolute must they get some self-motivation and start taking responsibility. They are beginning to realize that you are about to take off to a new level. They can see it and it is scaring the HELL out of them. Without you around, they will be sad-mad, lost, angry, depressed, and downright lost in their world because without you they believe their life is nothing. Watch them because they know you well enough that they could easily throw you off your game if you are not careful in the next couple of months. Be careful around them as you go to this new level.

You have done your duty with them. They will either SINK of SWIM this week! Time for you to go to another level with or without them. If they want to go then they will make a choice and show UP with MIGHT because that they want more out of life. If not, they will be right where you have left them this time next year.

No more.....SAD SALLY and SAD HARRY! Time is of the essence either get on the MIDNIGHT TRAIN OR GET LEFT THE HELL BEHIND. CHOO CHOO!!

Simplify your life and you'll immediately feel less stressed. You only need 3 of everything you got. That's why you have the father, the son and the holy ghost.

I am so glad my cousin taught me about the importance of self-evaluating my POOR PRIDE on a daily basis.

This has changed my life tremendously. You see, sometimes when in life we must realize that poor prides keeps us from becoming better than our best. Trying to stay in that box that people have put you in is doing more HARM and GOOD for your life and mine. I am not saying that we should beat up ourselves everyday about not being OKAY with our life. I am only saying that poor pride keeps us from doing better than we can do. I don't care how old or young you are there is always something standing in the way of you going to a new dimension in life.

Financially, I want to be free of this debt that I have accumulated over the years. In order to do this, I decided that I have to do better with what I spend my money and how I spend my money. It has been a struggle to stop the poor pride spirit that has become apart of me in the 39 years of my life. Not sure when and where it all started but I am freeing myself daily and it continues to be a struggle somedays.

But now, I have no problem with any of the following:

- Seeking Financial Aid programs that benefits me and my family, if and when I qualify

- Accepting advice and strategy on Financial Literacy as well as managing/budgeting money

- Saying NO and HELL NO when your gut feeling tells you to RUN FAST instead of doing what make others feel GOOD. My opinion matters the MOST!

- Saving up until I can afford things I need instead of running out to put things on credit just to get it over with immediately. There is POWER in delayed GRATIFICATION

- Buying off brand products to save funds

- Spending less on things that some may consider THRIFTY

- Living like the Bynums' instead of the Joneses

- Reciprocating with people who are AMAZING like me

- Affordable car instead of a car that looks good but maintenance is not up to date

- Coupon shopping and looking for thrift store deals of a lifetime

- Not looking the part just because of what people think I should have and what people think I should be doing because I have a husband, 3 kids, house, and etc

I don't give advice I just share stories. I'm becoming my grandmother. She tells stories that allow you to think critically then find a solution that fits you and your situation best.

Truthfully speaking you and I aren't happy with the shit we are seeing on a daily basis. The truth is that only we can change what we see. Nothing wrong with wanting more happiness and less sadness in our life. We have survived so much and now this!

Maybe it's time to move to a small City in China or either Bangladesh.

That backwards thinking is not helping us in anyway. Time to change up.

I've had two of my babies all natural with no drugs no epidural or nothing. I can take pain.

The stuff I'm seeing and experiencing with my eyes is causing pain in my soul.

People suffering in silence is painful. Thank God for allowing me to help birth what's bothering them out of their souls.

Your voice is what the world needs to hear.

I learned from my sister that some need simple encouraging words to go to their next level and others need to hear a reality check to go on with their life.

Know what people need. This is the key.

It took me 39 years to realize my True Value, self- worth, and realization that I'm a powerful force of nature.

I thank God for sending me exactly 7 people who have touched my life in a special way this particular year. They know who they are. They truly added value.

I'm no longer lonely and looking for others to complete me. I complete my damn self.

I used to do it for the likes but now I do it to get s*** off my chest. This is no longer a popularity contest. Y'all really helping to test chapters of my eBook. The posts that are good will get expanded on.

I have to admit it does feel good to see certain people throw a like on it. I know they feel me and what I'm writing is something that they have experienced to.

2   Poor In Spirit

A friend of a friend lost her daughter to leukemia recently. She journaled her thoughts. One message really touched my life. Basically it said nothing else mattered once she found out her daughter's diagnosis. All that mattered was time with the one she loved. Wow. I hear you God saying make the exit strategy a reality as quickly as possible. July 24, 2020 may be too late. You see - The people I love can't wait to have my full attention.

As she left for greater opportunity, she inspired many to set their personal and professional goals HIGH.

This is for you if you feel defeated. You are what you think and say. You are more than a CONQUEROR. Just when life seems to be taking a turn for the worse then there comes confirmation to keep stretching to become better than your best. Love you!

This is for that one person who feels like they should be doing better than their best. Your job is not fulfilling your ultimate purpose and your team does not reciprocate your awesomely ways. Your family and friends have no clue of how to assist you with your goals.

All you know that it is time to do something different. It all starts with focusing on the present and your future. Ask yourself today, where do I want to be by this Friday. Each day this week begin to celebrate your accomplishments. Be fearless, push yourself to be better, if it doesn't scare you then you aren't uncomfortable enough. Try this! Thank me later!

Your friends or family members are either jealous or inspired. It takes a lot to reach the inspirational stage for people who knew you when you had nothing.

If you got a business then teach someone else how to start theirs. You know that's why they hanging around trying to get clues.

You can't keep a man/woman until you value yourself plus keep your own house, car, and kids clean. She/He can't add what they don't see in plain view.

It is so funny how people will put things in a text message or DM on social media that would never EVER in their entire life come out of their mouth.

Why text things you would not normally say or ask of me in a face to face conversation?

Don't use technology to be someone who you want to be!

Just be yourself and stay over there with that foolishness!

Some of us sleep really good at night thinking we apart of the solution in making America Great Again. Really and truly our daily activities are feeding into the bigger societal problems.

The solution to the problem is YOU~! Look within yourself to get to the root. Facing that inner truth will free yourself and the world will be a better place.

To the people who might be losing hope. Just when you think that everything is shot to hell then bam there is someone who has gone through worse. In spite of you wanting, needing and ready for relief out the current situation. Just know that it will get better soon. I just want you to know that God is showing you all this so you'll have a powerful testimony to share. It seems like you might be the only one having a hard time but the truth is everyone in your circle is going through something. No one I mean no one has a perfect life. If anyone tells you anything different then just look at them like this o_O and walk away.

There is inspiration and aggravation. Some people move like molasses in they a$$es with no sense of urgency at all.

A recent survey found that COGIC members are the most healthiest citizens: daily activities for each day of the week plus ALL DAY SUNDAY and last but not least whole body (I am talking from head to feet) praise dancing.

Some stuff I don't even share because sometimes it is best to keep some stuff to yourself. Most times people are happy and excited for you outwardly but on the inside your victory, achievement, success, and change for the better is eating their insides up. Be careful who you share your dreams with because they could be the ones plotting out a plan to ensure it does not happen for you. Keep it on the low.

So many of us are suffering in silence. I am constantly looking at your pictures and can see it in your eyes. I know and realize that the majority of our circle is hurting just as much if not more than we are hurting. Your writings are cries for wisdom for your current situation because you are searching for clues on how to get relief. Truth is you are the answer to your healing from hurt. Just ask!

Financial hurt. Church hurt. Childhood hurt. Relationship hurt. Employer hurt. Family hurt. Just ask the poor in spirit about hurt!

Most people will just tell you to JUST pray about it. But if their leg was broke and hurting (worst pain ever) would you tell them to pray about it. No, you would call or take them to get help. There is a time for prayer and a time to pray using your feet for swift action. Just ask!

Don't be too busy with life to forget about the power in asking the right person for help.

You are worth more than you know.

Truth is it is going to get worse before it gets better. Take time out to get help today. Just ask!

They want your success but ain't willing to put in the work. You make it look easy. Hard work + Resilience = Your Legacy

That moment when your healed depression becomes another persons' inspiration, motivation, encouragement and empowerment to start their healing process! Today it happened!

The solution to the problem is YOU~! Look within yourself to get to the root. Facing that inner truth will free yourself and the world will be a better place.

Everybody wants success but only a few have the discipline, strength, mental fortitude, and grace to withstand failure.

The average fail and decide to never get back up to try again. They stay in that low defeated place for the rest of their lives. They have yet to realize that their failure is not the end. Failure is an option as it's up to YOU to choose life or death. Stay down and death creeps in slowly but surely. Get up and try again at LIFE.

Only the few successful ones, decide to dust themselves off, get back up and try it again and again until they get it right! Never giving up is the only choice YOU have. If YOU are reading this message then you are among the select few who dare to dream, hope, believe, and desire more out of life.

Success is in your DNA and that's all you need to know. Time to step it up a notch and stop worrying about what the average-minded people will say about you. You MATTER! Don't allow them to hold you hostage for another day. Break free tonight before morning light.

Wake up and do a high karate kick in mid-air to get your success and creative juices flowing!

Last night, I was so stressed I exercised for 30 minutes straight. Best 30 minutes of my week. I am sure my blood pressure went from 999/1000 to 120/80ish.

I felt so much better after I did leg lifts, high karate kicks, arm lifts, deer dance moves, and acted a plum fool DANCING all around the house with the kids dancing around me.

After it was all said and done, I felt better. Sometimes in life we must learn to dance in the storms - this was EXACTLY what I needed to get my HAPPY juices back flowing. I am a little sore this morning but all for a great reason. Best way to lose weight for me is to get up off my ASS and MOVE!

Eating snack cakes like the world is ending tomorrow, not walking because I don't want others to see me SWEATING while trying to loose what has taken years to gain, and staying complacent with my weight because people have always seen me as Tonya the BIG girl. I don't want this LIFE I want better.

I decree and declare that my MIND will line up with my BODY.

IT IS ALL MENTAL - IN MY HEAD: I AM FIT AND FIERCE!

No longer can I talk about it - I have to be about it YA'LL!

Some folks like to make things so complicated!

If I notice you are starting to make me feel like I should have known something but you don't immediately start breaking it down for me to understand then I'm going to shut down and walk away especially if you hear me telling you I don't understand what you are saying. I hear you but don't quite follow up.

This means explain this logic in baby terms, please.

Focusing on how far you and I have come is sobering as we think of things we have yet to see, hear, say, do, and go in life. Go easy on yourself. You have time to do it right. Celebrate how far you've come so far. Try not to compare your progress with your peers. This is the key to living your best life!

Some of us have judgmental friends that we can't, won't, and don't share our complete life with because their nature is to judge instead of empathize. They aren't perfect and neither are we but it's lonely as hell being in their company. Trying to have a mind blowing conversation with them leaves you feeling empty. Life is too short not to share without a care.

I appreciate all my nonjudgmental friends family members who let me be myself. They have a special way of listening and helping me to see life in a more interesting way. They are our real MVPs.

You are powerful because of what you have endured. Most folks aren't able to take much so they live a life of nothingness. You have withstood the unthinkable. For this, you are being rewarded with loneliness. Take it to God because only she can, will, and does understand.

Your mistakes make you GREAT! No one on earth will be able to heal that part of you that feels unhealed. Start healing yourself TODAY!

Looks can be deceiving...it may look one way but believe me it ain't what it is cracked up to be. YOU have a very good life! Stop comparing your situation to theirs. This is the key to your inner peace, happiness, and joy in your soul.

Just tell them the truth. It's a little uncomfortable at first but if they are who you think they are, they'll stick around afterwards.

Every time I give, I'm looking forward to positive karma working in my favor. I may not see an immediate return when I give but I feel like something great is in store for me and mine. Thank you in advance positive karma. You see, I gave from my heart, soul and mind today. Exactly 10 people were blessed because I showed up and showed out.

Not always about $$$ so sometimes it's the sharing of wisdom, spending time, and resources to get the people where they want to be. That's true priceless value.

Every time they think of you they will immediately think they are winning too. It's how you make them feel when you are around. You bring a different perspective and every time you step into the room the atmosphere changes. You are powerful beyond measure.

Life is what we make it. Dull, boring, good, bad, happy, sad, great, or full of excitement - the choice is all yours.

What's it going to be this week?

People need to know they aren't alone. The days of silent suffering are over for us! Let's get it off our chest so that we can breathe the fresh air blowing by. Holding all that in is only going to make you feel like passing out.

Do you want to pass out or not? If not...

Inhale. Exhale. Breathe. Live.

There will be people in your life who want what you got but aren't willing to go through what you had to experience to get where you are at.

Encourage them all you want to but they have to be ready to put in the work.

You can't possibly want it for them more than they want it for their self

3   Sugar Daddy

He wanted nothing more but her. You see she was a rare sight in his eyes. She had intelligence, the body chiseled for childbearing and when she spoke her people were healed. To get to her he had to approach the elders first. For they were the gatekeepers to any young girl becoming a woman. He sat amongst the elders, they quickly learned that he in fact had a plan, vision and needed his equal to bring it to reality. They approved and then he courted her openly...To court meant he would make her smile without a single touch. She smiled as often as the sun shined. As day turned to night...they longed to be together. He wanted nothing but her for she was necessary for the vision to unfold...they called her "Essence"...

Men will try to control you by playing games with your mind. Life is too short to be under the impression that what you are experiencing is love. To be honest, if it has been more than three years and he hasn't mentioned making you his then he is basically looking for you to take care of him until he finds a wife. Ain't nobody got time to be playing wife for a man who ain't trying to get his shit right. Every woman should consider their value today and say R.I.P. to the dead friendships and relationships that don't make you feel your best. That's the MF tea you needed to hear so he can stop playing mind games on you. That pussy lick down is only a temporary fix when you are looking for a permanent solution: a HUSBAND to call your own.

A lot of folks ask me what is married life like and I simply tell them like this...

If you move from job to job when things get rough then you probably won't make it past the first three years. You see, marriage is similar to a job. You have a responsibility to be there on time, to work at it daily to perfect your craft, and most importantly to do your work plus some.

Let me break it down...

Time - you wake up and go to sleep with the same person each day. They are the first person you see in the morning and the last person you see before bed. You spend lots of time with them and start to learn their patterns of behavior. Their ups and downs plus their good and bad sides. It takes time to get to know all of these things to see if they work in your favor or make you angry as hell.

Daily work - now most of you can't keep a job so it is nearly impossible for you to deal with stress. It takes work to stay married. You see, all days won't be like the wedding day looks. Everyone happy, blowing bubbles, taking pictures, you smiling and he smiling like ya'll gone live happily ever after. Naw, get those thoughts out of your head. It is some real work involved because there will be days you want to throw in the towel and say the hell with all this. So if you not used to dealing with stress on a job then I say you probably need to take some time to work on yourself before getting into a marriage. You will be tested each day.

Your job - It is a must that you give 100% not that 50/50 that everybody talks about. Sometimes you will have to carry all the load plus some and vice versa. Get ready to throw out all the thoughts of what a woman versus a man is supposed to do in a relationship. If you love your spouse you gone do any and everything that needs to be done plus some. Get ready to get your mind set on doing your part plus theirs. Shit happens in the marriage and it is all up to you on how you will handle it. If you ain't used to working hard and picking up the slack then go sit your ass down somewhere and work on yourself first.

This message has been brought to you today by a married woman approaching her 13 year anniversary. It ain't been easy but somebody has to do it. For the most part, he has made me a stronger woman than I ever imagined possible. I used to be very different and now I am better than I was 13 years ago.

She thought he was playing mind games on her but the truth of the matter is that she played the game on herself. Her situation was not because of him but instead had everything to do with her mindset. Years of pain had torn her spirit down. She began to let herself go sinking deeper and deeper into her very own sunken place. You see, she allowed what was. She had the upper hand, she had the financial ability, she had a go-getter spirit, and she had a passionate voice filled with the wisdom of life lessons. It was past time for her to step out on faith and take the risk of gaining more. After all, she had lost so much and therefore had nothing more to lose. With everything to gain, she set out to be true to herself. This was her time. Nothing else mattered more to her than the next mind game she was playing on herself. The game was named...Operation Set the Mind Free!

Everything with teeth is looking for love.

Truth of the matter is that LOVERS don't bite YOU.

Your love life should never be a secret. Your loved ones need to know who you are with. - 20/20 Cold Murder

You are either leading or being led by your loved ones.

Where are you leading them?

Where are they leading you?

Love makes you do strange things!

It is wise to only have sexual relations with the person you would want to spend the rest of your life with. One drop of sperm from them on the right ovulation day could change your life forever.

4   In Hell vs. Inhale Stress

I hear all this talk about providing prevention and treatment programs for the Opiod crisis but what about this new K2 and everlasting CRACK epidemic I see taking out my friends and family members.

When it hits home to one of your friends or family members then it is a CRISIS but until then the minority and less fortunate will suffer...

Warning. I've noticed that more of my previous coworkers are not minding their busi-ness. Hope you enjoy getting to know me better. I write my thoughts and feelings as this is my journal. Feel free to mind ya busi-ness if this was not what you were looking for. No hard feelings. Much love...

This is the second week of school and most teachers have already decided based on behavior and manners which kids will pass and which will be in the school to prison pipeline.

Do you know where your kids stand with their teacher ...???

5 Signs of a parent who is too busy....

Doesn't attend orientation

Does not email teacher with contact information

Does not drop kid off on time

Does not review materials inside of the backpack

Does not call up to the school to ask questions

Recently at work, one of our system servers shut completely down. The root cause of the problem was linked back to too many connections. This is profound.

Sometimes in life you will experience no connections, limited connections, and way too many connections. When you have way too many connections it tends to be overwhelming especially if the connections are taxing your system resources (i.e. your mental and physical health).

I have found myself in a position where I had way too many connections and I simply did like the system. I shut down. It is okay to shut down but during the rebooting process assess the connections before re-establishing a direct link. May need to MONITOR and rethink each and every connection then set up some guidelines, protocols, processes, and procedures to prevent another system SHUT DOWN.

Moral to the story: Choose your connections wisely.

Some parents right now sitting at home stressing their self out, eye balls rolling into the back of your head, blood pressure sky high, head hurting... thinking about back to school outfits, hair, nails and shoes instead of worrying about going to get the basic school supply list which will costs $30 or less to purchase if you didn't wait until the last minute. Time to get your mind right! Start washing, ironing, and getting a new pair of clippers to work with what you got already!

Waiting on them to reciprocate what you give so freely is like waiting on gas to be $1.29 again. It just might happen but chances are a whole lot of war has to go on before the prices drop that low. My point is they gone have to go through hell and high water before they become better than their best. Life is too short to wait on them to get their shit together. Meanwhile back at the ranch you could and should be focusing on things that bring you inner peace, happiness, and joy in your soul. Let the nonreciprocating folks kick rocks. Leave them where they be and simply focus on getting yourself together. You are worth more than you think but you just don't know it yet.

I used to have high blood pressure until I realized how to speak my peace and do as I please. I feel so much better getting shit off my chest and am in no way, shape, form or fashion concerned about what YOU or anyone else feels about my mission in life.

All those years I held things in did my blood pressure and progress no justice.

Now, my blood pressure stays at 120/80. It is only slighted elevated when I try to focus on people pleasing...

Have you ever been diagnosed with high blood pressure?

Are you a people pleaser?

If the answer is Yes to both of these questions then listen to how I healed my blood pressure...

Start telling people how the hell you feel...once you follow this treatment plan you'll immediately feel better! Save yourself starting today...

We need to stick together my ASS, someone needs to leave the pack!

Leave them and GO off and explore a path less traveled. It is all about self-discovery, exploration, and risk-taking in order to go from good to GREAT. Bringing others along too early can ruin the exploration because they won't see the path like you see it. After all, GOD gave you a unique mission on the path and you won't be able to explain it to them. It will be a waste of time trying to give them the clues that GOD gave you. Plus, you don't have all the clues you need to make it work like MAGIC. On top of that, there is no time and you don't have the extra energy to focus on anything other than refining YOU. Their opinions, complaining, grumbling, fumbling, and utter shock of the new path will merely be EXTRA NOISE. Get rid of their noise and focus solely on the mission at hand. That is your ultimate responsibility and nothing else. GOD is going to whoop your ass if you mess this one up because he has already blessed and healed you of the PEOPLE-PLEASING SPIRIT.

Quit trying to help everybody and focus on the fact that you need HELP, ASSISTANCE, and so many things to get your life, mind, heart, and finances straight. No time for nothing else!

You aren't there yet and you don't need to fake the funk like you have made it. Those false signals and PREMATURE ECLIPSE-LIKE LIGHT are going to be the death of your DREAMS, HOPES, DESIRES, and GOALS.

Sometimes we get so caught up in wanting others to go where we are going that we lose sight of the fact that we are in the wilderness and haven't quite figured out the key to not getting ate the HELL up by the animals in the wilderness. When you are in a new field of work, new relationship, new situation, a new job, or anything NEW it is very important to focus on being observant, learning survival skills while paying attention to clues for THRIVING, and certainly being focused on the traps that could send you back to where you were before - THE OLD.

Your nuggets aren't for everyone. Never waste time, money, and energy on people who don't want what you have to offer. Life is too short to be focused on them and their negative energy - instead focus on perfecting your God given talents, skills, and abilities. This and only THIS will make room for you to get you what your heart, mind, soul, and essence desires out of life.

GO ALONE and tell them the TRUTH you haven't figured it out EITHER!

I yearn to make a difference...

Little by little I am learning that it is really and truly all about the small things in life that lead to the BIG PICTURE. I remember the time when I used to feel like nothing was working in my favor and life wasn't getting any better. I worked two jobs and was always working to try and get ahead in life. Now, my hard work is starting to pay off. I have gone through so much to get to where I am today. If I told my story then most of you reading this wouldn't believe it. You would probably be like, "Tonya, you always seem so full of positive energy I didn't know." The truth of the matter is...I have trained my brain to not get bogged down in my past and the things that I have done wrong. I only focus on the good in my life and the good I try to bring to others. As I get older, I am starting to realize that the more I step out and work my faith the better I feel. At the age of 39, I am becoming who I was created to be... pure EXCELLENCE. It has taken some years, storms, trials, and tribulations to get my mind, body, and soul to where it is today.

This post is for you if you find yourself feeling like you are not making progress. The key to seeing your vision come true is to quickly assess how far you have come along in the past 10 years. You are not where you used to be and aren't around the same people you used to be crazy about. Things are changing and you don't even really see it. Take some time to quickly assess how much you have grown. This assessment will serve as motivation to keep you going. Stay focused on what you want to do and STAY READY. This will make all the difference in the world...Realize today that you are what the world needs more of. Feel good about who you have become and the rest will take care of itself...I promise.

I remember a time when I felt like I was dying slowly at work. I was helping others but really and truly I needed help myself. I needed someone to give me some advice on how to get my life going in the right direction. One day it dawned on me that no one was coming to save me. I had to take action and save myself. You see, I had the talent, experience, and genius but I lacked the most important asset: COURAGE! I mustered up all my strength and took a step that has changed the direction of my life in the most dramatic way. I put my fishing pole in the water to see what would bite. I smiled when I pulled my pole up out of the water and CAUGHT THE BIGGEST FIVE FINGER OF MY LIFE - A NEW CAREER in a different field that aligns with my life passion - CONSULTING. If it can happen for me then it can happen for YOU. Try putting your fishing pole in the water for a new relationship, new friendship, new career, new affordable car, renewed HEALTH, or simply a new way of living.

As I get older it seems that people my age and younger are experiencing their first stroke.

The struggle is real and the stress is at an all-time high. Time to get real about how we are feeling about our life. At one point, I had high blood pressure because I was doing too damn much. Trying to be everything for everybody until I realized that if I died then they would learn to do what needs to be done. This was a game changer since I love people but realize many folks like to use me. Free yourself today if you have high blood pressure you must learn to accept and apply the I don't give a FUCK attitude. Your veins, capillaries and arteries are going to thank me for showing you exactly how to release that life pressure. We all know that pressure at a high capacity will buss a pipe! Strokes can be prevented in many ways and I'm here to tell you that all that stress you are under is doing no good in your life. Get free today and stop allowing them no good people to worry the hell out of you! Tell me and we will come up with some I don't give a FUCK mantras that will help you get off those blood pressure pills because you have a new coping strategy. No more holding in that anger and shame!

Time flies when we are having fun. The day drags out by the second when we are in a pitiful state of anarchy. So glad my days are just beginning to fly by. Bye bye to uncontrollable anarchy been there done that before!

Everything that you have experienced in your life has prepared you for what's ahead. Today you'll see that your presence, style, naturally fun spirit, mannerisms, and niche for excellence in your work bring about more favor.

Have fun and enjoy each stage of the process.

5   I Am Not Stopping

Unstoppable is what we are!

Yes, we have had our fair share of disappointments in life. We have dried our tears and then some. But TODAY is a new day. We will live and not die realizing our dreams are all we have to go by. If we stop dreaming, we begin to settle for status quo. Average people are okay with what everyone has.

We want more out of life. On top of that we are willing, to be fearless. No more holding back. We are all in or nothing. All in on relationships, our career, our business, and most importantly our financial well-being. We realize today that our resourcefulness will bless us with the freedom we desire.

Freedom is what we want and that's what we will get. Solely because we are willing to put in the work to get where we want to be. You're hard working attitude, dream oriented mindset, and spiritually discerning ability when it comes to people is a gift working in your absolute favor.

Time to look up some stuff about the ideas you have. After the research is done, go into ACTION as if the world is ending tomorrow. The key to our success is having a sense of URGENCY about the belief, hope, desire, and dream. Take it easy for what! I see now that these problems are all opportunities to work FEARLESSLY at motivating GOALS.

I remember a time where I would wake up early and not want to post anything on here because I didn't want others to know I was awake and on social media early. How silly of me! Now I don't care. I am up early sharing my thoughts, ideas and epiphanies. These nuggets are eye openers that will help get your mind right in the a.m.! That's called morning coffee...

Seasonal friendship is your friend.

There comes a time in life where you begin to see the value in cutting people off. Their mind stays in that sunken place and you have tried to tell them to RUN when they see a spoon and coffee cup combination. Instead of running, they curious about how far the sunken place will take them. You see, the running gene in their spirit has yet to be activated. It's going to take time for them to decide what they want out of life. Two choices for you:

1) Keep reminding them about the coffee cup and spoon combination that triggers them to go deep into that sunken place

2) They must have an innermost desire to see their feet in this situation. Having common sense to run until they are in a safe place to collect their thoughts.

This #2 takes mental fortitude that sunken place people haven't activated.

It's one thing to have ideas and another thing to have the resourcefulness and courage to get the shit done!

If and when you are not educated on the system then please believe that there are very few people who are going to come to your rescue. It is a must to know how the system works. This is the best way to navigate your way to success! Ignorance of the law will leave you and me feeling RUN over!

We need system educators to guide you and me on what's happening and what's not happening in our favor.

This dawned on me today when the man said this is "private property".

It is not just one thing that will lead you to take action. It's a series of things that all push you to simply do it. The tipping point is near...

Some of us are so damn hard on ourselves that it is stopping us from going from good to great. In order to reach our next level in life, we must learn to be patient with ourselves. No one can be harder on YOU than YOU. You are a great person, you have come a long way, and you are destined to change the world for the good. BUT, the only thing is you and I are going to have to take a step back, take a deep breath, thank GOD for where we are in our lives today, and stop beating ourselves up as if we don't deserve better. We know we can do better be we are the only ones holding us back - NOT THEM it is YOU! Get out of the way SELF!

Access to credible, specially-tailored, and quality resources is the key to having a great career and amazing quality of life.

When answering my phone I always start off by saying 'hello tell me something good'!

This has worked in my favor because it immediately commands that the conversation be high level. Try it and thank me later.

6   Are You Okay?

Ten things that bother myself and most folks but we have to be quiet, sit down and be HUMBLE...

1. Access to Higher paying jobs with benefits

2. Quality education with niche training

3. Student loan debt and still overqualified

4. Professional development opportunities

5. Valuable Connections to Changemakers

6. Debt from credit cards - financial illiteracy

7. Bread winner status within the household

8. Business owner without access to capital

9. Family income disparity... Enuf said!!!

10. Friends who truly inspire and support.

Bonus...Flexible time for work and family life!

Okay...here's your homework if you are bothered!

Step 1: Find something you good at and people want to buy.

Step 2: Google your states' Secretary of State office and find the articles of incorporation to file your business name.

Step 3: File for your free IRS tax ID

Step 4: Get money!

Step 5: Keep a notebook until you start getting more money than you know what to do with.

Step 6: Call Jim Sadler with Score Mentors of Little Rock to ask him quality questions about how to become better at business. Find him via Google.

Things I notice while out n about with three kids:

Folks telling me I have my hands full

Assuming I'm unwed

Asking if the girls are twins

Smiles

Stares

Are all three yours?

Folks testing kids for manners or ratchedness

Me teaching while I shop & listeners ear hustling

Until you get your mind right, it is okay to send their calls straight to voicemail. Wasting your precious time and energy for what. No need for that. To be honest, they don't make you feel good. Just stay focused on your goals and don't focus on them so much. They can go to God just like you do. After all, what they going to do when you completely decide to uproot and move?

Maybe they'll share their story to start the healing process today.

I was in a situation that I thought was hopeless. It dawned on me just the other day how I could turn my life around. I had to stop being angry, forgive myself, meditate on ideas, and strategically plan a BIG GIRL move.

Public service jobs are all day everyday focused on helping others. I worked in public health for nearly 13 years. I have to admit that I forgot that if I helped myself first I could actually begin to help more people. The public really wanted to know how I have applied all that book knowledge. It was when I learned the art and science of storytelling through Toastmasters, APHA leaders Dr. Camara Jones, and Dr. Adwele Troutman that I began to help more people.

This morning I'm waking up thanking God for ADH, APHA and my network of public health professionals who have all played a part in helping me to help myself.

Put simply, share your personal and professional story to guide someone out of the rut their stuck in. It works every time.

Great morning!

Unforgiveness does a number on your mind, soul, and body. Consumed with thoughts of what happened, what should have happened and what you wish would happen is what keeps your mind focused on all the wrong things. I have found that in times when I can't forgive them then I simply focus on forgiving myself for the role I played in the situation.

I tend to overthink everything I do because I want everything to go just right. So when something unexpected, unplanned, crazy, or down right off the wall happens then I tend to be stunned, numb, and paralyzed in damn near shock in awe. So now, I have learned that I can't control what other people do but I can control how I deal with others who are blessed to be in my circle. I am forgiving myself for the part I played in being the fool, the part I played in loving way too hard, and most definitely the part I played in trying to help folks who take me for granted. Their loss and my gain.

Today I forgive myself so that my mind, soul, and body can move in peace until I can muster up the mental strength to forgive them.

When a person is dealing with sickness in health, marital problems, death in the family, trials and tribulations in life and at work, family demons, struggling to find a job to take care of their family, relationship issues, or just in general being overwhelmed in life...THEY ARE LOOKING FOR YOU TO SAY AND MEAN THESE THREE WORDS!

I LOVE YOU

Today is my 10 year wedding anniversary. To be honest, I'm truly happy this year. There have been years where I wanted to throw the damn towel in and move to Tijuana, Mexico to start my life all over for a fresh start lol. Yes, there have been ups and downs but that's life. I'm not perfect and neither is he. Two imperfect people becoming...I'm glad I met him at Kroger on Oak Street Conway and asked him for his Kroger card and he asked me for my digits lol. From there the story unfolds...

Shout out to all those who are married or have been married. Only you can relate to me when I say, "I'm truly happy with MYSELF this year".

Nope no pics because I don't want the haters to cast an evil spirit on what I got going. So... Just imagine me and Calvin smiling this morning as we take care of not one, not just two, but three beautiful kids who will grow up knowing their mommy and daddy tried to be the best example of a mom and dad who made it happen through thick and thin!

When you make a person mad who has been disenfranchised and/or treated unfairly then you catch hell plus some. It is best to do what is right upfront to let them know you understand their concerns and are working night and day to rectify the wrong that has been done. In spite of what you have heard, there is no telling what hell you will catch by not putting ketchup in the bag if fries are ordered. This presents a problem because the disenfranchised understand that they aren't getting the same resources that others are privileged with.

There was a time when I used to work so hard at work that I never had the desire, motivation, drive, or the interest to go home and start planning my exit strategy. I would get off from work and be so drained, tired, and un-motivated from pouring all my energy and time into doing what was good for others.

It took me over 12 years and a little encouragement from a Nino Brown motivational video to make me see that I had to realize my own dreams by planning, working on the dream, and executing the my goals to get where I wanted to be.

This is the key to changing our future in the direction that we want it to go. Hard work pays off in a special way when and if you work for yourself and realize your goals matter just as much as theirs.

Stilettos or flats?

I used to try to wear stilettos and nearly kill myself trying to walk in them. Now I know my place in life is in flats. No more falling for no reason for me. I ain't got time to be way up in the air trying to impress people by showing them how strong my ankles are.

My nickname is Tonkepooh and I admit that my ankles are the weakest part of my body. I get this from my daddy! He calls it an ruptured Achilles tendon!

7   Mindset Strong

Looking for clues from all the wrong people will leave you clueless. Just imagine.

The older I get I am starting to realize how much I don't care what people have to say about my way. What happen to my people pleasing spirit?

What if we spent time cultivating our friendships by telling each other how we are inspired by their life, work or love of family? That would make a huge difference in this world of very amazing but unrecognized people. Much love to the people who received a personal note from my heart to theirs. Look forward to connecting our stories to make a greater impact...

Your marriage is going great, you have your dream job and are at the height of your budding career, the kids are all growing and helping out around the house, your family is doing well plus they check in on you and don't want anything but to hear your lovely voice, and your friends adore you and never take you for granted.

What more is there to life when you have all of this?

Most folks don't add co-workers because most of them think just because you make one or two messages that you be on social media all day and night not working on work stuff.

They just need to mind their own business. Focus on their mouse cubicle and not yours. Am I right? Can somebody, anybody testify?

If your coworker had an eye booger, what would you do? Keep in mind that you are the new kid on the block. Got to lay low for 90 days...

Folks that constantly bring up your past want to keep their foot on your neck. Don't allow them to hold you down any longer.

They remind you of where you were but never acknowledge how far you've grown. They know your old business but don't know your new BUSYNESS! Ha!

This is for those who can't let it go. Truth is...the past is when YOU felt the happiest so your mind stays in the past. Too bad for you.

My present is a PRESENT and my FUTURE is so bright I must wear shades to dim the light.

Come on now. Get a life! Let this be a reminder to you before going back in time to bring anything up that might be funny to you but is hurtful to me or others.

Let me go eat my healthy lunch!

There are some folks that will celebrate your success and others who don't have it in them to celebrate with you. They are pretty much miserable and aren't really motivated to be more than average. That's okay. Leave them alone in their pity party before they drag you down with them. Help them by getting yourself established. Your success will leave them clues I promise. Plus God don't want you to take their whopping. That's exactly how you feel after dealing with them for more than 30 minutes lol. Chest pounding like whew...I need to RUN.

When you find people who are achievers and want to celebrate and support your goals then cherish the hell out of them. Those folks understand reciprocity well. They are rare.

Let us get that REM sleep that we need to finish the week strong.

Yesterday, I attended parent orientation at my son's school. I couldn't help but to notice that I was a minority. A saw a few other folks that look like me so I smiled and spoke to them just to ensure they felt comfortable and welcome. Having worked with, been around, raised with, and lived around all types of people I felt like I was in my element. As parents, we must learn to show up and get out of our feelings about racism, etc. Just know that racism exists and learn to operate in a strategic way to guide your child through the SUCCESS pipeline. In spite of my son, attending a majority white school, I plan to support and encourage him to be the BEST at any and everything he does to learn, grow, and excel in his own way.

I am teaching my son to be a leader and communicator in any environment you are in. He saw his mother and little sister support him in his educational journey. That alone put a smile on his face. The icing on the cake was when he saw all of his friends. That is really all that mattered to him.

I guess my point is...when you are outnumbered then just be yourself. Don't be afraid to ask questions and definitely BE AMAZING in spite of being outnumbered~! Remember that kids don't get all bogged down with the same things parents see, feel, and realize.

In addition to child-hood bullying, some of us know and have experienced bullying from adults. Adults in our family, in our social circles, and especially those in the WORKPLACE.

If you are a workplace adult bully, please GET A LIFE outside of work. You're are causing more problems than you know.

Suffering in silence is what you have been trained to do. They say you a strong woman just so they don't have to do anything to assist you. You can handle it, there is nothing God can put on you that you can't bare, and this too shall pass. These are all the things that they will tell you when they are really saying shut up, you don't matter, and stop bringing attention your way. No more suffering in silence for me and the people I love. If you hurting say something, if the people around you truly love, care, and respect your value then they'll make you a priority and listen to your story. Strong women don't have to be so strong when they have real friends and family who care. What they really are saying is pipe it down because I'm weak and can't take much more! So hush up until I can get my life on track...

Fear is to be conquered...

The only way to conquer fear is to have a vision then act on it. You see, you must not get caught up in the rat race in your head. That's called analysis paralysis where you start to overthink your very own thoughts. The over thinking is an action in your mind but doesn't cause your body to move along.

The key to conquering your fears this week is to set goals. Setting goals causes your mind to open up a bit more. This week, I set a goal to make a difference in 10 people's lives through the art of writing, speaking and research. This means I must touch at least two people per day.

Best way to conquer fear is to take action, have a sense of urgency, and stop people-pleasing. Charge full speed ahead and don't look back because a split second of doubt could cause a total loss of achieving the goal. Nothing else matters more to you than your GOALS. That's the motivation you need to be fearless in the face of mediocrity.

Sometimes we need to do a factory reset!

My $30 Android phone has been acting up for the past week or so. I decided the other night to do a factory reset to get the gremlin out of my phone. I lost all of my contacts and pictures. So yesterday, I posted my number for my close friends and family to reconnect with me. One person called to check in on me to see if everything was okay with me to say hello.

I had a chance to call her back this morning. We had the most thought-provoking conversation - talking about everything from friends, family, business ideas, work, and basic life shenanigans. To say the least, I felt so much better after talking to her. She even said, "LaTonya, I knew you professionally but now it is good to hear from you on a personal level. We need to go into business together because you have some great ideas on your mind. Lunch soon?"

That made my day. I love talking and sharing my love with people. It feels so good to have deep, thought-provoking conversations with people who want more out of life. It inspires me to continue to try my best to enjoy life and the little things.

I wish her all the best in her life and I look forward to doing lunch soon. I am sure it'll will be awhile with her schedule going like it is. She knows who she is so there is no need to tag her.

Moral to the story: We should all try picking up the phone and calling a random friend/co-worker to check in on them. It can be a life-changing experience for you and for them. It might just be the conversation they need and you needed to take your life to the next level. My factory reset lead to something amazing!

Speak with authority as if God herself is using you to reveal the next set of plans. We must no longer be afraid of what we see. Living in a tent will be much better than continuing as is. The social condition of your people is only getting worse by the day. They keep you fat and happy so that you remain complacent in a mental comma about your surroundings. As you learn to train your brain, you will quickly start to see the reality of our situation. One by one wake them up and notice some will die asleep. Let them be because you will quickly find others who can awake them in a way that you can't. This is the key to inspiration and truth telling that people want to hear and see in their life.

Keep doing what's right. What you do when no one is looking matters the most. You can sleep in peace tonight knowing that you did what comes natural.

When a loved one dies. A part of you dies with them. All of the things that you have shared and the wonderful conversations are only memories. There is no one on this earth that can ever replace them. It is healing to know that I can continue their legacy by being for someone else what they were for me. This is where healing starts as I grieve the loss...

It may not seem like it right now but YOU and I are both making an impact on the people who come into contact with us. Their lives are forever changed by what we say, what we do, and they will always remember how we made them feel. Realizing this is the key to having a great day.

As leaders, we must recognize that we have come a long way to get to where we are now. It certainly did not happen overnight.

It took time, blood, sweat, tears and then some more to be able to speak, think, and do things the way we do. We must not be so quick to challenge others to have a sense of urgency as they discover their true nature. Everyone has to go through their own process. No need in rushing it but instead encourage their growth each step of the way. Who knows you could be the tipping point for them in going from good to GREAT~!

Passion + Action = Kick Ass Behavior

Mindset: Find out what skills you have then package them in a way that is easy for others to understand and find them valuable.

An encourager encourages because they understand what they needed at the time when they were going through pure hell.

Today is encourage an encourager day.

Who is there to encourage us when we need it?

Look within. The good Lord is the ultimate source.

Feature on phone!

One of the most important features on my phone wasn't working properly. I tried and tried to make it work but it wouldn't. Today, I decided to uninstall the feature and then reinstall it using a new way.

I am happy to report that the feature is now working.

Moral to the phone feature story:

1. Sometimes we must stop trying to make things work that aren't set up correctly.

2. It may be time to uninstall or disconnect from things that aren't working in your favor. You may lose some things but what you will gain will be working like you want it too.

3. Be careful when choosing new things. Make sure it is the right one you need in your life.

4. While you are working through the process of getting the new thing set up - be sure to pay attention to the settings you choose. Putting in the wrong information could be the problem you had the first time.

5. Don't waste your time trying to set it up the same was as before. Try a new way the second time. This could be the key.

6. A new way of doing things makes your life much simpler. Less headaches, less time spent on trying to make it work properly, and more time enjoying life.

Features Matter!

8 Straight A & B People

An education teaches you to function in this system. Wisdom will teach you how and when to leave their system and create your own.

Educated people are not a threat to the government. More education often leads to analysis paralysis and NO ACTION. This is for you if you have thousands of dollars of student loan debt but nothing but a job to show for it. Time to apply the models, theories and principles to real life situations lived daily. Starting with YOU and your household.

Some people with degrees get the BIG HEAD and only want to share wisdom on social media. They really want to signal to others that they are smart. Oftentimes smart people can alienate themselves by always flexing their smart muscles. We are all lifelong learners. I learn more from people with no degrees because they tend to get straight to the point. We all know that one educated person that will complicate the hell out of everything. Sir...Ma'am if this is for you then sit down and be humble!

And one more thing...most educated folks are too proud to apply for government assistance. They qualify but won't go see about getting some help until they get truly established. Food stamps, SSI, Disability, Medicaid, WIC, Rehab assistance with education, and daycare vouchers are available. This is confirmation to those who are too proud or prideful. Drop a note below if I'm missing anything that will help somebody.

More education is good only if you are setting yourself apart within an industry where you are respected or you see a niche for your talent. Quick question: Have you applied the knowledge from that first $30,000 degree you still paying off?

Truth is: You just creating more debt because you secretly want and need validation from your peers. Let me save you money and a headache.

YOU matter! Say it to yourself 100 times until you actually believe it.

Teachers are preparing for kids who need hugs and love from their career focused parents. Quality teachers can spot a child who feels love and gets quality time at home. Teaching is easy when the kid and teacher both speak the same language. Love is a language!

People on my team with a high school education making a killing in the technology industry. They have IT trainings and certifications out the wazoo.

Let me get to work on catching up with them!

Got all that education and still unhappy? Time to take those nervous nail biting hands of yours and use that keyboard/phone pad to apply for a new job. Probably in a different field since you are most likely black balled in your current profession. Yep I said it...don't be mad at me. Be mad at yourself. Happy Friday from me to you~!

Got all that education and still unhappy? Time to take those nervous nail biting hands of yours and use that keyboard/phone pad to apply for a new job. Probably in a different field since you are most likely black balled in your current profession. Yep I said it...don't be mad at me. Be mad at yourself.

Don't enroll in another school. Just need to reinvent yourself with the Masters you already have. Save your money and R.E.I.N.V.E.N.T.!

There comes a time in life when you say FUCK this shit. You stop the analysis paralysis and just do what the FUCK you feel. Realizing that it is your life to not live in the past or dream too much about the future but instead BE IN THE MOMENT. Time is the only thing you have. Spend it wisely doing those things that make you feel ALIVE, WELL and HAPPY. If you are living a mediocre life for others then you are definitely a people pleaser. That spirit has to die before you can, will, and do become better than your very best. So on today, repeat after me...FUCK that shit. Find yourself be true to who you are and don't let others stress you out. After all, who are they? What they got on you? What they got that you need?

Walk as if you are on a $1 million mission.

Something about these degrees keeps me boxed in...high school diploma, bachelor of science, Masters in public health.

In order to be who I know I am I must reevaluate what I know as truth, facts, and history. Weigh it against the current facts and evidence of life. Invite scholarly investigation as we explore new possibilities.

The Bynum method of research and scholarship will put me into the circles where I need to be. Being a cast out to the public health community no longer matters. In general, I set out to truly heal the DIS - EASE of what plagues the Arkansas man, woman and child. This test case is my purpose, plot, and passion for which I was birthed for.

Out of the box behavior will lead me to the cure. I start with self-reflection which leads to a new path of understanding what I thought was understood. An old soul I am and an old soul I'll be....

Average grades don't mean YOU are unintelligent but rather it notes a need for alternative methods of teaching to understand the subject.

Don't allow teachers and the midterm report to make you feel like school is not for you. You just need assistance with another way to learn the basics of the subject matter.

Our kids deserve to learn and so do YOU.

Stop the poor pride and ask for assistance with the lesson you are struggling with.

I have come to understand that all my degrees have yet to produce the courage, strength, mental fortitude, tenacity and will power to change the social condition of my people. Knowledge is power only if I learn to apply it wisely. This is the key to a degree. Degrees without training leaves us with only ideas and no action. Like Nike, we must no longer be afraid to fearlessly JUST DO IT!

The death of a black baby!

Before I had any kids or a Masters degree, I was very concerned about the following infant mortality statistic:

White women with less than a high school education experience less infant mortality (death of baby before it blows out it's first birthday candle) than Black women with a college degree.

Most times education leads to better health but not in this case, but why?

Public health scientists are trying their very best to figure out why this is happening...

Here are some of my thoughts now that I have 3 kids and a Master's degree in public health with some life experience under my belt...

1) Black women rarely form underground networks in which we share/reciprocate resources i.e. time, energy, wisdom, program benefits and $$$.

2) The black teen pregnancy statistic shames us even if we are married with kids. An underlying stigma falls on black women with children. This is a subtle stab in the psyche.

3) The black girl is innately strong and has charisma. We are groomed as young girls to be wise and learn to suffer in silence. This silent suffering ages our bodies on the inside in which our reproductive system undergoes cellular stress of a woman twice the age.

4) Since childhood we have experienced the Jerry curl, perms, and the weave. Our hair and skin on our head is affected by these products. Like lotion, these products soak into our system. Undocumented cellular changes are happening at a young age as our mother learns to care for our naturally kinky hair.

5) The black woman undergoes unheard of stress while pursuing her college degree. The stress of Independence, relationships, being the family's first, and lack of direction or guidance on how to properly navigate the college system is stressful.

6) First baby aborted syndrome. The next baby (FIRST BORN) has to grow in an unhealed toxic internal environment of shame, pain, hurt, anxiety and depression.

7) While growing up, Black girls are touched inappropriately, raped, and molested by family members or friends of the family. This affects all body systems internally. This diminished value harms the Black Girl Magic that is needed in this day and time.

The list goes on and on...these are some of the reasons I think our babies die before they turn one year old.

Yes, I said it. Just need to research it a bit more to find documented evidence. The silence and lack of discussion around these 7 points is killing our chances of thriving and no longer merely surviving.

The white people will never acknowledge or validate you for your good works. Better recognize the people who look like you who are rooting, cheering, and supporting you along the way. They can't respect you until you start respecting yourself. Focusing on quality rather than quantity will shift your mindset to see what matters the most as you WIN!

Educated folks have a tendency to complicate the hell out of things that are easy to explain.

A plant can't fully grow to its' potential inside of a box! In order for a plant to grow, its' roots must have the right environmental combination of dirt of the earth, water and nutrients to form a solid foundation for optimal growth!

9   Obesity Suicide

Facing her mortality she grew a steel backbone that couldn't be deactivated. She said what needed to be said out of unimaginable love for her people. Her flowers were brought to her daily...in a way Obesity had healed her mind, body, heart and soul. The sun would bring her first son and all would be told finally.

All her life she had suffered from overeating. Food was a way of easing the pain since she didn't want to hurt anyone. She had been hurt in a way that most animals don't prey on their enemy. Wow. She channeled her pain onto paper and speeches. The result was nothing shy of amazing. Her impact was unparalleled... Her new name was Fearless...

She saw the white powder donuts and purchased them for the kids to enjoy. The kids waited longer than expected so she found a quiet place and ate her heart's desire of the white beast crack powder donuts. After the high, she crashed and burned her dreams. Her dreams of successfully becoming better at health for her wealth depended on her ability to move quickly. She failed but got back up to try again. Next time she'll buy their favorite fruit for her quiet place.

I cured my own high blood pressure by telling the truth about my concerns. Now my pressure stays at 120/80 (normal). Keep that stuff bottled in if you want to and it will take you to an early grave. That bottled up beast inside of you will manifest itself as a health issue until you address the root cause. Tell someone who can empathize and forget the sympathetic. Lesson from me to you...

This is for that one person thinking about suicide. I want you to know that I care. You matter. Take it one day at a time. Seek out resources to get you well again by calling...1.800.SUICIDE

We need YOU around. Life won't be the same without you. Much love from me to you!

Drugs/Overeating, Gambling, and Women/Men - when people get way too stressed out they turn to one or all three. Shit just got REAL

At the ripe old age of 39, I have come to realize that repressed emotions of hurt, pain, grief, denial, and utter frustration from built up "stuff we need to get off our chest" is the cause of early disease and early death.

Ya'll ain't gone kill me so bear with me as I use my social media page to share my TRUTH. If you can relate then hit the button if not then carry on with your day.

My death certificate will list "UTOPIA" as the cause of death. It is a new ICD 10 code that I just created today. Somebody tell the coroner. Ha~!

Funny how MARRI-AGE makes it okay to be OBESE! Not okay for me anymore...

I am not on the market but that doesn't mean that I have to eat up everything in the market!

The other day my son told me, "momma your stomach is going down". I immediately looked and smiled at CJ and told him "Thank YOU". You see, he sees me at night before bed working out and sweating up a storm. He always remind me to take it easy. Sometimes I get a little carried away as if I can lose all this weight in one night lol.

He also told me that he is glad to see me exercising and he wishes that daddy would join me. I told him that we all have to make up our own mind about what we want and don't want in our life. He looked confused but in due time he will figure it out for himself on what I am saying to him is "Life Wisdom"!

Retraining my brain to exercise FIRST thing in the morning before touching my phone. Week 2 and I'm winning!

I used to get so carried away with how big I have gotten until I realized this. I can work on it each day. It is up to me to do what is best for me and my body. What I realize now is that I control my environment. This has been key. Being surrounded by love motivates me to want to walk, eat healthy more often, and work out so that I feel stronger. Each day is a new opportunity to work on my life. It doesn't take much to do what's right. YOU and I will be healthy if it takes us another year to get where we need to be. Work in progress is what we are!

The years of high blood pressure have been wiped away by a simple method of being honest about who I am, what I know, what I want to do, saying what I want to say, and going where I want to go. There is really no need to hold all of that inside. Like built-up pressure in a pipe I was headed for a stroke. Letting it go and being the true authentic real me has healed me from a life headed towards chronic disease and early death. I got s*** to do!

Me Too! The Obesity slowly creeped up on me as I tried to hide myself away from others who might see me. You see, I figured if I hid myself then no one not even him would see me or want me. It took 35 years to discover that it only happened because I was accessible. I ask myself for many years, Why Me? Going over and over and over this in my mind has killed precious time, energy, and unrealized dreams.

No more comfort food eating to hide the pain, shame, guilt, and heartache from what I am overcoming. My story matters. It is the key to ending this problem in my family and yours.

Seeing any fat girl with big clothes on or jacket will forever send the sign to me. She is hiding and the silence is killing her slowly. I recognize her because she was once me. Me too! Is what I say to her so that she never feels that she has to suffer as long as I have. Silence will truly kill her spirit. Her voice is powerful!

Holding in all that hurt, anger, pain, shame, guilt, depression, and disgust is killing who you could potentially be. You must forgive yourself first.

Today, I forgive myself for the things that I have done in the past. I want a better life and I want it today! DAMMIT, I deserve to move on.

What's stopping you from your dreams?

The answer is "YOU".

Survivor guilt is a mental condition that occurs when a person believes they have done something wrong by surviving a traumatic event when others did not.

Dear Obesity,

You have been with me for far too long. I felt you creep up on me as I suffered my first painful life experience in childhood. Only you truly know how to hide me and who I really am inside. The comfort food, bad memories, and adult body shaming all work as convenient way to keep you as my life partner. Each day I battle to get rid of you. With every disappointment, storm, terrible news, and continued reminder of that day, I am reminded of how we became lifelong friends.

Lately I've been working to end our lifelong friendship. I realize that if I am to truly rid myself of you for good I must go back to that painful day. That day I felt that I allowed pain, hurt, shame, guilt, and depression enter my life and my body became the welcome mat.

But today, I am mindful that it is not what I am eating but instead what exactly is eating me. It is you Obesity. You and I will continue to talk until you are gone forever. Until then, I'm simply saying hello Obesity in hopes of saying goodbye Obesity soon. I am welcoming HEALTH. Stay tuned.

Please share if you know of anyone who can relate to this letter! Be sure to tell them you are there for them because you care. Wishing all the kids, parents, grandparents and caregivers a great year of school. I used to always wonder how some kids were made cum laude and always get 1st place in everything. Now I realize, it is really their mindset plus they have a great support system. Their support system makes it natural to put education first. Supporters ask about and are involved in the activities that they are excited about. Get excited about what they are excited about then you'll see them on a path towards their own version of success.

That moment when you're healed depression becomes another persons' inspiration, motivation, encouragement and empowerment to start their healing process! Today it happened!

Eating for comfort!

Had a doc appointment and found out I'm 345 lbs. I credit this to stress, not putting myself first, eating on the go, and generally taking care of everyone except for myself.

So...

I'm happy to report that I am working towards a healthier lifestyle. Because I have a sedentary job, I now realize that I don't need a lot of calories. This is week 2 of eating oatmeal, apples, oranges and drinking lots of water. For dinner I eat pretty good. Before bed, I make sure to do some form of exercise. Vacuuming, 10lb weights, or leg lifts. I got this! Looking forward to looking down to see my toes and not my stomach. Slow and easy will get me towards health. My health is my wealth.

Why is it so hard to put yourself first?

While studying for my Masters Degree, I began to study depression for my final paper. To be honest, I really didn't want to study that topic. It was given to me by my mentor, Dr. B.! Depression wasn't something people talked about so I didn't want to study it. One year later, I'm still studying Depression and working towards the final touches on a paper I should have wrapped up last year. No motivation really to get it done.

I've been in that low place for several months leading to years of shame, guilt, defeat, and a feeling of doom. I've constantly had to use self-talk to get myself up to go on another day. People see me as happy go lucky but the truth is I put on a good show. After the show, I come home, eat unhealthy, take my high blood pressure meds, and do my best for the kids, snap like a snapping turtle at my husband and go to sleep tired then wake up tired. That's depression y'all.

But now for the past couple of days, I am starting to see a glimpse of light and hope. I am on a path towards doing better. I have support and I feel better than I have ever felt. I left a very well-paying job with BENEFITS to start a new career in a totally different field that I know absolutely nothing about. I felt myself dying slowly in my previous job. People pulling me in way too many directions, mastery of my daily tasks, and a general feeling of what's next. For the past several days, I have chosen to speak life over my mind and body. Thank God for my friends and family who have supported and loved me. Don't know where I would be without them. That's the truth! They know who they are...our long talks and thought provoking conversations were the therapy I needed but wouldn't seek out professionally. I didn't want to look like I needed help because after all I am supposed to be in the helping others profession of "public health".

Today as I think about the graduate paper and all that I am studying it is apparent why I chose Depression chose me I didn't choose it. You see, I have a story that needs to be shared with the world. If I can heal from depression and high blood pressure then the world can heal too. Many chronic diseases are reversible! Now the paper has purpose that I didn't want to admit at first. Until I tell my story, the paper won't be a quality paper that I can really and truly consider as my first author paper "The Role of Depression in Effective Chronic Disease Management".

Why are so many of our friends and family members depressed and/or sick with high blood pressure, high cholesterol, diabetes, COPD, and asthma?

My new friend at work just offered me some of my favorite chocolate brownies and I declined. This is week two of trying to do what's right for me and my health.

Self- talk: Mornings are only for my fruit and oatmeal time. Learning to say No when I really want to be a people pleaser and say Yes. I lead when I say No. No telling what type of stress he is under. I can relate to eating sweets for breakfast. Been there and done that before. Sugar high takes me low later.

If I knew early on in my life that this overweight, dark skinned, uptown, unpopular black girl from Spa City was going to be whom I am today then I would have sat back, relaxed and continued to pursue excellence in my own way. But now, God blessed me to be 39 with stories to share, connect and inspire my community.

Being over 300 lbs. is no excuse to stay that way. Never too late to break terrible routines or bad habits that are not working in your favor. Take it one day at a time. Learn to prepare ahead and love yourself.

Once God has blessed you to eat, see, touch and taste romaine lettuce it's hard to go back to iceberg lettuce. Life is all about believing you deserve only the best quality L.E.T.T.U.C.E.!

10 Truth Triggers

If you are my friend then you are definitely someone who I speak to and want to hold a conversation with. Would even have lunch with you if the opportunity presented itself. Smile because you are my friend~! That alone should mean a lot to you.

There is always that one coworker that finds happiness trying to make everyone else miserable. Filing grievances left and right because their personal and professional life sucks like octopus tentacles.

One more thing... Folks over 65 should not be in leadership positions. Reason being...they have a tendency to be complacent and relaxed when it comes to addressing status quo issues that are root causes of the social chaos in this world... Need more youth mentoring programs for a serious revolution. That's why I enjoy mentoring so much using my personal and professional life as an example of what works and what does not work. The youth need transparent mentoring...

Many agencies, departments and businesses close as a result of arrogance. Root cause...Someone doesn't feel validated in some part of their life so they see themselves as the go to for any and everything. That is really sad for their coworkers and fellow leaders who have to pick up the pieces afterwards. Amazing leaders inspire others to see their unique value and assist with their personal and professional development...

Must beware of folks that constantly talk about God and Jesus. It's called hyper-religious. I luh God too but can you tell me how you are applying those scriptures to your life. That's what will help me. Something going on behind the scenes that you not telling. What happened to you?

Want some stress in your life...mention race, religion or politics!

People get in their feelings on these topics. I love intelligent dialogue supported with facts - that's how I learn.

To be honest, most of us are all one paycheck away from being like the homeless people we see in the mornings with that sign. Truth is you don't want to look at them because you see a lot of yourself in them. Turn your head the other way if you want to. Try to position your car just right so you can't see them.

Reality check: stop buying things trying to impress people who don't care about you. That debt is leading you on a fast track to homelessness.

Work towards your financial goals one day at a time.

Aim to be that one person in your circle that says exactly what everyone is feeling but no one can put it into words.

Some folks get all worked up over politics. It is not that serious when you think of yourself as a politician. We all have a platform.

I love love love Nino Brown and Love Dorsey videos and posts. They both give me life. If the videos you watch ain't stepping on your toes then what you watching them for.

If they say they love you but you still feel empty on the inside. Own the truth. They hate your ass and could care less about your feelings. They love to play mind games because they know your human nature seeks love and attention. That empty feeling will go away when you build your self-esteem and self-confidence to own the fact that you have survived what puts most people in the fetal position. Love yourself out of emptiness. All the quotes, sermons, texts, and phone calls don't matter if you don't know how special you really are

I will write until I inspire, motivate, empower, and encourage someone out of low self-esteem and low self-confidence. I have been there and understand what it takes to see the light in yourself. It all starts with hope and belief that you can become better than your best. Take it one day at a time and you will soon experience progress towards your goal of thinking highly of yourself.

Be sure to surround yourself with inspiring, motivating, empowering, encouraging people, videos, and stories to help build you up where your strengths and lessen the fears about your weaknesses. I have found great joy in being around people who are the epitome of love, I also enjoy watching videos by Nino Brown one of the best gangsta motivators who tells the truth in the most odd ways possible lol. I also find Jim Rohn give great life philosophy and career advice for personal and professional growth. I love Toni Robbins, Les Brown, Brian Tracey, Lisa Nichols, and last but not least Love Dorsey.

I hope these folks can help you come out of that dark place that you are in. It will and can get better and it all starts with you believing in yourself, doing what you love, and stop the people pleasing spirit that has you trapped in a vortex.

Feeling overwhelmed but I'll clean one room at a time. I have all weekend to get it back like I want. DHS wouldn't approve of what I see right now. My personal life will align with my professional life. Say what you want but we must learn to sweep around our own front door before helping others...

On social media but house looking like it needs more attention than my social media friends.

No longer is it okay to look the part but we must teach what we practice at home...

Does your home align with your social media posts on success?

As a new mother, I always thought that it was important to educate my child. After all I knew I was his first teacher. I taught him the ABC song but didn't understand the importance of phonics. He knew the song but didn't know the sound of the letters. Sounding out the letters is the key to reading. Teach your kids the sounds of the letters and watch them grow into early readers. If they can sound out letters in a word then they can read. After they learn the ABC song your job is still undone. Phonics Matter

In life, we want to do what's right and what feels good but sometimes we forget what's important. For most of us we just don't know until someone points out the key. Early readers are leaders.

Growing up I wasn't the most popular; I can appreciate it now.

The popularity seems to do something to the kids who are in the spotlight.

From what I see, most of the popular kids didn't have what it took long-term to master the social pressure. Some led and others were lead into a life filled with chaos.

God has blessed so many of us not to be found in our States Department of Corrections database.

Don't be judgmental like you have never did anything wrong. A lot of us have been sparred if we tell the truth aloud.

I know I was headed towards juvenile delinquency back in the day. God woke me up right on time. He sent me through for a reason so that I can relate to the youth who feel lost and confused about their importance in the world.

I'm here to tell you...You Are Important and it's not too late to turn your life around. Let that soak in...

11 She Weird

Good night to you. If you are having trouble falling asleep because of your current situation then just reminiscence on how we met and how much I care for you. Sleep peacefully. You matter!

Parking as far away as possible is revolutionary.

My classmates have babies that are graduating high school - congratulate yourself for this accomplishment. I have two girls still in diapers and one graduating kindergarten.

This definitely has me thinking... I thank God for financial stability and a help mate. My hat goes off to my classmates who survived the struggle of raising a leader!

Rest in peace to all the worms that didn't make it to the other side. This heat is relentless to all of us.

I'm the type that if I see a worm struggling I pick it up and fling it off the sidewalk and into the grass so that it'll live.

Yes, I'm going to heaven for that alone. Saving worms should get me into the pearly gates. Right?

Nothing like a scalp massage when you have a deep-thinking brain drain career.

I am retiring by age 40.

Now, please return to what you were doing. I just needed to put that into the atmosphere so that my marketing committee can help make it happen.

Things I remember from high school:

Doing sentences

Walking the circle after lunch

Driver's Ed & permit

Riding bus 42

Wearing wind pants

Wearing Nike everything

Taking Spanish I, II, & III (Reagan)

Teacher's aide

Diamonds in the Rough

Playing the flute - 1st chair

Being a gangsta nerd

Senioritis

Things I remember from cashiering at Kroger:

Long line with my fav customers who wait on me

Those morning donuts before the flies lit lol

Crispy strips and mash potatoes for lunch

Clocking in and out with my finger print

Coupon crazed customers

Big ass dog food and 24pk pops. HEAVY!

Banana code 4011

Going to LR for customer service training

Introduction of Uscan

Mrs. Warren

Folks stealing meat

Speaking Spanish with customers

Please make your final selections at 12

Sore feet and back hurting

Dreaming about scanning groceries in sleep

It may be uncomfortable at first but work towards addressing all of your sisters and brothers as they are. Sister and Brother!

Must have a touch of psychosis to become a fierce business owner. This is not for everyone especially for those who wear their heart on their sleeve. Sometimes customers will not like your services and other times they will LOVE your services. Take it all with a grain of salt and keep the mission in mind. Each customer is a lesson learned... I appreciate every last one of my customers.

I am that person that will go and sit in the white folks section of the room and wave to other black folks to come on down. There is no reason why we should be still sitting in the back of the room. Hey if the conference organizer or speaker calls for audience volunteers I want to be front and center, Johnnie on the spot. Can't see me way back there so I need to be up close so that I can see, hear, and experience what is being said and not said.

The more we tell, share and discuss our story of how we have overcome our very own life struggles the more we will empower others to keep pushing until they meet their goal.

We can do it if and when we decide NOT to give up! Giving up is not an option but rest is only okay if you are working your assets off.

I remember a time when daycare and mortgage was eating up the budget. Had to rethink the situation.

Stay at home moms or dads are amazing!!!

Can't wait to go to sleep and wake up to work on my dreams and help my kids start their businesses too. Never too early to get them thinking about their first LLC.

I love fall. Mosquitoes gone, flies gone, nice weather, and it's not too hot not too cold. Everything is just right to sit outside on the porch to enjoy life

We inspire each other to step outside of the box into the place where we are supposed to be. Maybe this new place is box less!

I've heard the do it for the dick and pussy challenge, so here is my written version...listen up...

This is what I will do for the DREAM... It is my daily challenge, I go hard for the D...meaning my dream! The P is for the PASSION for the DREAM!

I wake up early for the D

I motivate my 5 kids for the D

Support my husband and his D

Celebrate 10 year marital anniversary for the D

Call my mom and dad daily who enforced the D

I will speak for free to reach the D

Build my network daily for the D

I'm writing a book for the D

I journal daily to see progress towards the D

I mentor successful people for the D

Listen to NPR for new insight on the D

I support others in reaching their D

I go hard for the D

I take my kids to the park to live the D

I focus on my goals for the D

I practice reciprocity and truth living for the D

I am working magic at DXC for the D

I ain't depressed about the D

No longer living misery because of the D

Cut family members off quickly for the D

Small friends circle for the D

Stop watching TV for the D

Got Google chrome for documentaries on the D

I perfect my brand for the D

I earned my bachelor and masters for the D

I sit back and study successful people for the D

I love telling my story to reach the D

I switch it up daily for the D

Make the routine like gravy for the D

I make folks think and believe in their D

Aaaaaaayeeeeee!

What you gone do for the D?

Your DREAMS matter!

Get you some DREAMS and your life will have meaning!

12 Wake Up

Really need seven streams of income to say all that needs to be said...lemme stop until I get to where I need to be. Don't won't to come up missing you know there are body snatchers who would love to see someone with revolutionary tendencies fall off the face of the earth. Back to being diplomatic as my friend says...

I go back and forth on the village mentality of raising kids. I've seen some folks that feels that it's okay to chew up food then feed it to the baby as if they are helping the baby. No way Jose. Where they do that at? OMG stop that. Smash it up with a fork or don't feed it to them at all.

Too much smoking, drinking, having sex and eating unhealthy is all a part of you trying to escape your reality. Accept the present. Better choices lead to better results. Never too late to decide to do what needs to be done.

The elders don't want to mentor you because you think you know every damn thing. Show your listening skills instead of your speaking skills. You'll get to where you are going a lil faster. Trust that wisdom comes with experience. Keep bumping your head for no apparent reason.

Headed to a professional conference dressed like you going to the club afterwards. Put that outfit back in the closet and save it for the bedroom. It is frowned upon silently. Only your salary will suffer behind it. Dress for success. You are a leader not the life of a party!

Some sit on the sideline waiting for the main squeeze to fumble the ball so they can run the interference play. If you fumble recover quickly so no touch downs are scored.

I had to move from Spa City to Conway to go learn something at UCA. Truth is yes it took me five years to graduate but I graduated. Best decision of my life. In college, I saw opportunity and met people who looked at things very different than I did.

You are loved. Don't give in to the pressure. It takes pressure to make the shiniest diamond. You will shine after the transformation is complete. I promise. Smile while you going through. It takes darkness to truly appreciate sunshine.

Probably need to stop going to lunch with those who make the same or less than you AND/OR stop having lunch by yourself sitting in your car being introverted and anti-social. Try going to lunch with the group who makes more than you do. That's why your weekends tend to suck because you do the same thing each week.

Next week, should be your week to take a person out to lunch who makes between $25 - $50 per hour. While at lunch don't talk about other people at work, office shenanigans, or small talk. Try talking about personal growth, dreams, their succession plan, retirement programs, and professional development resources.

Don't act like your nosey self can't locate who makes what in the transparency or company database.

Time to flip the game on them. You'll be twice your age before you wake up and realize they ain't going to change. You have to change. Change how you deal with them, change what you demand from them, and change what you require from them. Sometimes change is what we need to wake the fuck up out of a terrible situation. Life is too short to stay unhappy in a job or relationship that doesn't make you feel awesome. Flip the game today and thank me later!

Black people wake up and realize that when we start having real mind stimulating, mind regulating, and healing conversations then we will be those Kings and Queens I have read about. Until then, we will continue to exist in our dysfunction. Yes, some of us have made out good but until we all are happy none of us should feel like we are successful. Share your story until it touches and compels your people to RISE to the occasion. Everyone has to realize and believe that they were born for a reason. No one is a mistake. Black people are great! Yep I said it! Walk taller, speak with authority, and don't take no shit. Call it like you see it every day of your life. That's the key to good living.

I see another problem with us when it comes to dealing with school officials. You see, my child goes to a predominantly white school. This means that on a daily basis I am seeing folks that don't look like me. His teacher is white but I have absolutely no problem with communicating with her via email or face to face.

Some of us are very intimidated by school officials and/or white folks for one reason or another. There should be absolutely no reason in the world that they make you feel any type of way. Their number one priority is to educate your child. Your number one priority is to support them in their effort. Now that you know that then the next step is to find out how your child is progressing with the curriculum (stuff teachers teach the kids).

Ask your child about school, his friends and his teacher to see what's going on. If you notice anything you don't like then you have a right to rectify the situation until you are satisfied. Parents are not the problem they are an important part of the solution. Have confidence in yourself, ask questions, and speak with authority as if your tax dollars are keeping the teacher paid. The teacher is earning her way and you must let her know as often as possible if you are happy or sad-mad about your child's progress at school. This is the key!

If you work in customer service, please check your facial expression, tone of voice, body language and attitude. It is not the customer's job to take your shit. Be grateful to the customers or find yourself without any.

Trying to get an oil change and that's all I need from you ma'am. Sorry your life and career sucks geese eggs!

It takes prison to appreciate true freedom. Nothing like getting a phone call from your family member who is locked up in the mental prison they created for themselves.

Wake up call for me!

One day you'll wake up and work on your goals rather than theirs... That's when your life will start to unfold like never before...let that sink in

The dream will bring about doubt!

If and when you want to have something that is rare or unheard of you must be prepared for the self-doubt that will set in. On top of self-doubt, there will be people who care for you that tell you to give up because they don't want to see you hurt or disappointed. If you can program your mind to see and think past doubt then you will be one step closer to bringing the dream into a reality.

We have what it takes and eventually we will celebrate the dream. Never give up because of doubt!

Kids are in school and parents are working to have a good quality of life. Time is flying by as we work towards retirement and high school graduation. If we aren't enjoying the process then it will all be for nothing. The process is what makes the success all worth it.

Black leaders have so much to consider as they wake up each day of their lives. It seems as if the weight of the world is on our shoulders at times. We must continue to do what is right, just, and unheard of. Our moves must be strategic, calculated, and well-thought out because we are playing chess not checkers. The game is to empower more leaders no matter what. The challenge is to groom, mentor, role-model, and affirm a person's presence in the world. Being the go-to-person in your house, at work, or in the community makes you a leader. Responsibility brings about leadership. This is the key to understanding that leadership gives you a platform to display your true nature to make a difference. What difference you make is all up to YOU and me!

Four car tires!

Our lives are like an aired up car tire or flat tire. Some of us are riding around on a life donut.

If your car tire is aired up then you feel like you are spending quality time with your loved ones, you have a career that is manageable and you like your annual salary, and your spiritual growth is blossoming by connecting with like-minded people who practice/apply what they learn.

If your car tire is flat then you'll feel tired of your loved ones, your career sucks and your salary puts you in line with all of the financial assistance programs. On top of that, your spiritual life is in need of spiritual resurrection.

If you are riding around on a life donut. You stay mad about your family, friends, coworkers and your spiritual life is near death. You have hit rock bottom and it's hard to get up.

Truth is that all cars have four tires. You may have one tire fully aired up, another one flat and two on donuts. We must learn to check our car tires on a daily basis so that we can arrive at our destination successfully.

How are your life car tires looking?

13 Glow Up

Tomorrow is my first day on my new job. I'm excited about this new journey. Went back and forth for a couple of minutes of how to wear my hair on the first day. I've been natural since 2007.

So I take pride in my coils. I finally realized that how I carry myself and how I wear my hair is my personal brand. This brand worked in my favor for going from secretary to Senior Analyst. Therefore, I believe and trust that it will take me to my next level. My natural hair says...LaTonya Bynum is intelligent, fun-loving, valuable to the workforce, unique, and most of all she knows how to research then analyze AI (artificial intelligence) when trying to find the root cause to the issue at hand. Yep my hair says a lot. Lol.

Prayers are most welcome as I start my new profession tomorrow morning in Conway! Wow.

Day 1 was a success. I'm going to enjoy the full fitness center, FREE WiFi access, tv lounging station, kitchenette/dining area with freely furnished coffee, snack/refreshment center, onsite daily vendor run cafeteria, spacious parking, basketball court, ping pong ball tables, fools ball, on site shower, walking trail, flexible schedule depending on account, telecommute option available eventually, resourceful team members, and excellent retirement and health benefits. Almost too good to be true. Wow. Is all I can say...

I was overdressed because everything is relaxed and casual at the office. I'll keep to my high standard so my works aligns with my dress. God has truly blessed me.

First project assignment came today in today to give feedback on a PPT presentation.

Thank you everyone for the well wishes. It worked out...stay tuned for more!

Sat at my desk today and nearly teared up thinking about the fact that my impact has gone from local (County adult surveys), state (statewide health surveys), and national (Rural Health programs) to now global (Electronic Data Interchange). Feels great to be able to use my experience and love for people to contribute to the growing field of healthcare information technology

Hint to someone looking for a hint: research technology related jobs available in Arkansas. Most of these jobs require two things: go-getter attitude and a minimum of a high school education.

Start with indeed.com. Look at the job description. Take free online courses that relate to the required skills needed for tech jobs.

Skills needed: How to use a computer and make the computer work in your favor!

Next up...let me research how to share my wisdom and insight via a podcast. Stay tuned for career tips and a glimpse into a day in the life of LaTonya Bynum.

This is for one person who is looking for a promotion.

Here's what you should tell your supervisor or colleague...

All my work is up to date. Is there anything I can do to make your job a little easier today?

Moral: Build skills, be resourceful and be fearless. You'll become the go to person if and when you add value to the team.

My birthday is July 24. I only want one thing from each of you. Do this for me pretty please, encourage at least three people each day then ask them to pay it forward the LaTonya Bynum way.

YOU ARE AN ECLIPTIC LIGHT!!!

They can't OUTSHINE you - YOUR SHINE IS SO FREAKING BRIGHT THEY NEED SOLAR ECLIPSE GLASSES JUST TO LOOK YOUR WAY. THAT IS WHY YOU GET SIDE EYEZ and NO DIRECT STARES!

The average salary in your circle is $35,000 - $54,000! Surround yourself with those who make the type of money you want to earn. The successful leave clues in what they say and do on a daily basis. Ask them questions and stop complaining about what you make to people who make the same or less than you do. Misery loves company!

Never thought I would ever get PAID speaking engagements for showing up just to tell others about my weird, awkward, old-fashioned, crazy, and not what is considered normal life stories.

The pay gap can end with you by using your negotiation skills. Conversation goes like this...

Let's talk benefits, perks and hourly salary rate. I'd like the Cadillac package of benefits, work from home flexibility and $33 per hour. I'll be awaiting the counteroffer. Thank you in advance for the consideration.

The people in your circle are being blessed just by the simple fact that you allow them in your inner circle. When your blessings are truly flowing they leave residue for others close by...

Today I will be having lunch with my son at his school for the first time. This is a really big deal for me. I used to work in LR which prevented me from being too involved in his school life. But now, God has blessed me to be less than 10 minutes or so away from him. I can't wait to have lunch with him. I want him to know that mommy and daddy are so very proud of him and all of his accomplishments so far.

Don't allow your friends, family or coworkers to hold you hostage and silence your powerful voice. Life is too short not to become better than your absolute best. After all, who are they? What they got on you? Are they paying your bills?

Let them stay sad-mad, complaining, and depressed about their life if that's what they want. Time to focus your attention on Self-care before you run your life into the dirt fooling around with them. Then who gonna come to your rescue - NOBODY!

Be honest with yourself today and get whatever is bothering you off your chest. It can't wait another day. Your transparency is the key to your next level.

Please don't change means...don't go higher because you might not be available to me anymore. They need you to cope with their situation but who do you have. You see, people are all different but their behavior is in a pattern. You see, they will always be who they are until you change. It's a lot to wrap your head around but the truth is. You must change because it'll take years, months, and days for them to love you like you need to be loved. Please do change... This is the only way to become better than your best. Over the years, it has been change that has excelled your growth and potential. Change by the second and don't look back...

If you have BIG ass dreams then don't play yourself short because the people around you are lame and don't want nothing out of life. You will be old and gray before you wake them up out of the deep sleep they are in. You are not Jesus Jr. Remind yourself that God didn't put you on earth to resurrect folks spirit if they have dry bones - that is a job for God himself.

If being around them makes your head hurt, stomach turn, and you start feeling dizzy when you see them then RUN the other way. They are wasting your time. Your time is precious. That time you talking to them and trying your very best to help them with their problems could be spent working on your plans, hopes, dreams, and aspirations in life.

You could be writing another chapter of your book. You could use that time to perfect your work. For some odd reason, you don't think that you have any value. So please allow me to remind you that no one is going to tell you what you should already know about yourself.

You are a rare jewel. When God make you he did not make a mistake. He set you apart for a reason so that you could be an ecliptic light. Being around all that foolishness has somewhat rubbed off on you. There is still time to decide what you want out of life. It is never too late to make your BIG dreams become a reality.

Why waste your time with nobodies when you are SOMEBODY special?

She think she all that and a bag a chips...

There are some people who can't and won't be happy for your success. It is not in their nature. They will stay sad-mad, confused, and downright hateful about any and every move towards success you make. Please don't get side tracked with their attitude, behavior, and dislike of you not spending time worried with them. The issue is that they really want to ruin your good life and all the fun you having. If and when you decide to leave them where they are at then you will begin to experience relief and an utter sense of HAPPINESS. You might find yourself walking around and then immediately do a high karate kick in mid-air then go back to walking...So much happier without them around but you know they stay ruining your good life.

If being around them makes hurt neck hurt, blood pressure go up, and it causes your stomach to feel like you got to boo boo then they are doing your life no justice at all. Time to re-evaluate your circle of friends and the people you call family. Sometimes in order to do something you have never done you have to do things that are out of the box, rare, weird, irregular, and not-so-normal to them. They stay having 1,009 questions about your moves. Only slowing you down. Get rid of them and make moves by yourself until you find others who on their path towards success. That is the key to staying motivated and eager to reach your dreams.

After all, you can always call or text them at any point in your life and they are still going to be right where you left them - COMPLAINING about they life and how the world is so messed up. I don't have time to listen to that sir or ma'am. You might need to seek professional counseling for the issues you are dealing with. No more wasting my time with foolishness anymore...sorry but now sorry!

Time to accept the fact that YOU ARE ALL THAT AND A BAG OF YOUR FAVORITE CHIPS.

Leave a comment below and tell me what's your favorite bag of chips.

I love me some Doritos'~! That is my bag...what is yours?

I'm convinced that to accomplish my next set of goals I'm going to search for role models instead of mentors. The role models may not be accessible but they can still provide clues to their success if I watch their ways, mannerism, walk, and talk. This is the key of how to be and how not to be as I find my own way towards freedom and liberation!

Make a list of your dreams then ask yourself what will it cost me to maintain the dream. This is the key to simple living!

I'm not saying that we shouldn't work but we definitely have an opportunity to do what our parents couldn't do. Retire early because we have access to the internet. We have the ability to learn anything we want to learn. Explore your internet with passion for renewed skills and abilities that show your value to the market.

The negative thoughts kept me in a place that I didn't want to be. I had to talk to that inner child within me. Talking to myself and feeding my mind spiritual, financial, physical, psychological, and emotional wellness made life better. Being a positive force of nature is a mindset. Daily struggle of becoming better than my best. Only God can take me where I need to be.

Lord bless our resource mindset and show us what's possible if only we believe. Show up and show out in our PayPal account.

For inner peace, forgive them.

You'll feel so much better. Life is too short to hold that against them. You are giving your power away by steady thinking about them and that situation. Instead take your power back by telling yourself to forgive them because they truly don't know any better plus they don't know who you are in God!

God hasn't forgotten about you!

When it seems like nothing is happening in your favor and everyone else is living in harvest and abundance but God forgot your deeds.

It only means that your turn is next. Be patient and enjoy your process to becoming better than your best. Have fun getting ready for the next level.

Celebrate with them because you will soon be celebrating too.

14 Dear Me

Sunday morning truth!

I've gone from saving the world to saving myself for the loved ones who pour into my soul. It took me a long time to see that it's okay to take care of myself. I'm not talking about hair done, nails done, vacations or purchasing items that make me feel better but instead I am talking about truly getting my rest, speaking my truth, cooking healthy, watching shows that elevate my thinking and being around the ones who I love dearly. It's the little things in life that bring joy, peace and happiness. I feel free and am ready to learn more about "Self-Care".

I'll leave you with this quote that helps me carry-on daily...

"Self-care is not selfish. I can only help people from a position of strength. I must put me first then give from a position of strength. Giving will start with my household first then move toward others areas of my life where I feel reciprocity working in my favor."

Dear Drug Dealers,

I really can't stand what you have done to my family and friends lives. To escape their past, they call, text, walk, wash cars, run errands, do small jobs just for you in order to get their next fix. Because of the fact that you like to feel powerful over people, you continue to serve them their choice drug. At night I'm not exactly sure how you sleep knowing that the last little money you accepted from them could have gone to that person's mom, wife or child.

Somewhere deep inside your heart it hurts you to see all your customers suffering. You call them customers to distance yourself from the fact that you are serving dope to your sisters and brothers.

I want you to know that I am hurt by what you sale. Since I was a young girl I stayed mad at you. As a grown woman, I'm still mad at you. When will you stop selling and do something productive with your life. I wonder what drives you. Is it just fun, a game, good money, quick money? I know something happened to you that you just can't understand. You are now addicted just as much as they are addicted.

It is in you to do something positive. You are respected by so many, yet you still feel empty. To heal your hurt, I am asking...no I am begging please start praying and speaking life into your sisters and brothers. It will heal your hurt. Your voice is more powerful than you know. Heal the people you are serving dope to. The skills you have built in this drug dealer game can be put to good use in the business world. Hell you already got a corporation.

Please stop because I really can't take it anymore. My family and friends are hurting. You can help me by speaking life and not serving death. I care.

Maybe it will touch at least one drug dealer's heart.

Slow down today and nurture your relationship with the secretary, janitor, valet and security guard. Just to put you up on game, these folks are the true gatekeepers of the agency you work for. To honor them simply stop in your frantic rush to your desk and ask them how is their day going so far. Be genuinely interested by working on your body language. They read people well. They know if you just want to hear the usual... Everything is going great... OR...if you really are interested in their day.

I have been in both a secretary and janitor position so I see how folks looked down on me. Over the years I've met some of the most amazing and down to earth people in these professions who are just like me. To be honest, their titles make people overlook who they really are. Most of them are simply retired from a long career in an amazing field, in school, others have had life circumstances to happen, and most are using that job as additional income to fund their dream.

All I'm saying is take time out to get to know a great group of people. They all have the power to make your life a living heaven or hell.

Piss any one of them off and see what happens next. You'll have headaches that you can't figure out why...paycheck late? Trash running over? Missing mail? Boot or ticket on your car? Bad reputation?

Honor the gatekeepers and you can't go wrong!

Dear Givers:

The takers in your life will never affirm you. They don't have it in their DNA, cells, mitochondria, or vessels to RECIPROCATE to the level you do. They are in your life to suck up all your energy, money, and time. You continue to allow them to do you that way because you haven't discovered your own value. God didn't place you on this green earth to be used, abused, and hung up to dry rot.

Once you wake up and smell the coffee beans then it will probably be too late. You are spending your good years with those who can't, won't and don't appreciate you. Learn to love yourself and then they will get a CLUE.

Signed,

I don't want to hear your complaints anymore~!

Dear Haters,

I know you like to get my attention so that I'm not focusing on what's important. When I had no goals, when I wasn't making power moves, when I was depressed, when I was approaching 400 lbs and when I was the unhappiest in my life YOU were a ghost. I didn't see or hear anything from you.

But NOW, that I am taking big risks towards my passion in life. Here you come to try to put doubt in my heart and mind. I can't lie you had me there for a minute. I had to get my mind right. Walked a couple of blocks and did some of my favorite deer dance exercises to take my mind off you. Had to kick off my dopamine levels (i.e. happy juices) and get those cortisol level (i.e. stressed the hell out) down.

So now, it is Friday give it all you got because I am ready to RUMBLE as they say in the WWF. You can't stop what God has in store for me. Your attention just made me finally realize that I am doing something positive in my life. Others are taking notice and are inspired by the change. I love every day of it at work, at home, and in my community. Stay mad instead of setting some goals for yourself.

I'm going to put you to work haters. Your new role on my team is to run the Public Relations and Communications part of my business. Thank you for your pro bono work. Ha-ha!

Signed,

Go run and tell that!

Dear Lord,

Send my single male and female friends a person to honor, love and cherish them for the rest of their days! They are ready to trust in love again. Only you know their hearts desire.

Dear Lord,

Put it on their hearts and minds to RECIPROCATE the value we bring, have brought and will continue to add in the lives of those touched. All friends, family and colleagues are blessed by the fearless example to speak life, honor YOU Lord, and share life wisdom. They will become better than their best because of the gift of RECIPROCITY.

Dear Lord,

Show them a sign that you haven't forgotten them. They need to see you show up and show out. Give them a break- through for their faithfulness in you. Comfort them to let them know they are truly loved.

Dear Lord,

Thank you for the favor. You are always fair towards me. I'm thankful for the burden you have placed on me. I know and understand that I can bare it all. Because of my strength in you and our long talks about my troubles and happiness, I can truly say without a shadow of doubt that you have set a path before me that only a few have walked. I can't tell it all and even if I tried too I would not be able to get the full point across. As I prepare to do your work, lead me, guide me and send me assistance, mentors both young and wise, and most of all let us forgive ourselves first and then forgive each other. I'm not perfect but I certainly strive to do, say, see, hear, feel and taste all that is good. I see you trying to get my attention with the recent storms of nature and life storms. I am awake in you this Thursday morning. Use me like you have never used me before. My arms are stretched towards you, my mind is open for a new download of the wisdom of an elder twice my age, and my feet and hands are full of praying action. Thank you in advance for favor and it is fair.

Dear Black Folks,

Just be GREAT and navigate the hell out of racism. Look towards the blueprint left by our ancestors if you are ever in doubt of how to navigate. Take fearless action to leave a legacy for your grandkids children.

Dear Lord,

Please use me and my transparent life to inspire, encourage, motivate, and empower 7 of my friends and family to step out on faith. This week will end with utter amazement and jaw-dropping stares at what seemed impossible to us but possible because of our belief in YOU. You are a way maker like no other. May our spinal cord be realigned to walk fearlessly on earth? May our vocal cord box speak truth to power and heal sickness shutting down healthcare systems due to lack of need and not a single customer present. May our feet, eyes and hands be used to go places, see sights and touch people who others can only imagine? Amen!

Dear Parents,

If you can't leave work to get up to the school then try the telephone or email to check in on your baby. Interim progress reports just went out - are you happy or sad-mad about your child's progress?

If you don't show interest then chances are the school will consider your child for the unofficial school to prison pipeline program. Look it up for yourself so your child doesn't become a participant in any pipeline programs.

P.S. Most schools have all types of ways to communicate with them. The phone, theirs email, and also most of them have social media pages.

The kids who get a quality education and the most scholarships all have involved parents who get up off their ass and make their child's education a priority.

I've always wondered how the cum laude and magna cum laude children's parents do it. They take their child's education serious and they have learned to navigate the school system.

We must learn how to deal with the majority white school officials. We must make sure our kids are not good but GREAT LEADERS prepared well for 21st century jobs and have the ability to run their own businesses.

I just want to be myself this week!

That's my goal but for some very odd reason, I feel stress and pressure sometimes to be what others need me to be.

A daughter

A sister

A mom

A wife

A grandmother

A coworker

A classmate

A friend

A business owner

A cousin

A niece

A mentor/mentee

Who God made me!

Being myself this week, means that I feel free to simply be who God made me. That is the title that's the most important to me. Nothing else matters more than that.

Dear God,

Bless the homeless during these cold winter nights. As we think about the homeless let us all be reminded that we too are only a couple of paychecks away from their same situation. The homeless don't want handouts they need a hand up in life.

We have so much to be grateful for in spite of the goals we have yet to reach. Grateful is a gifting spirit.

Amen!

Dear God,

Bless all marriages! Let others not speak on what they don't know or can't understand because every marriage is unique. The movies make marriage look all rosy poesy but the truth is that it takes hard work, perseverance, and a caring heart. Those who have never been married can't possibly understand what it truly takes to UNITE two people in YOU. It is a process that most will never experience because they aren't ready to be transformed.

Lord with nearly 10 years in my marriage this coming November 10, I credit all things to you. God you are the one thing that keeps us UNITED while enduring the UPS and downs! All of this and the prosperity is only to make us stronger to withstand the bull crap and gifts that life throws our way.

Dear Lord,

Help us ALL to focus more on our strengths and less on our weaknesses. You have given each and every one of us talents, gifts, and skills. Set apart from others is how we were made to be.

We are strong because of you and how you designed us. Magnify our strengths in YOU so that others see, feel, understand, and hear your clarion call to be GREAT.

Amen!

By the end of this year, I'm believing that God is going to guide me and send me three high-level top notch resources for becoming a full-time business owner doing what I love with a home office where I can home school my kids and be GREAT.

Big dreams come true with fearless action.

I decree and declare it is so.

15 Survival of the Fittest

She showed her mind and never showed her body. Her heart grew out of pain. Her name was adventure...

Do you and be yourself! Only focus on the conversation that builds your strength. In time you'll learn to quickly compartmentalize people into the A, B, C, & D groups. More on that later...

There is a BIG concern with the violence epidemic in Arkansas. The conversation at the capitol is...what to do with the thousands of unskilled out of work residents of Arkansas.

Officials are saying: put them in the pipeline to prison! Make profit off these people.

This is for all the church folks that think just because they pay tithes that they must have direct access to the pastor and his wife. Calling, texting and Facebooking at all times of the night and day. Unacceptable! They got a life too!

Your pastor wanted me to tell you. Stop calling him with that mess. Call on Jesus. Also his wife wants all the women in the church to stop calling her husband stressing him the hell out. Now, she got to pray and council her husband because you can't go to God on your own behalf. Also they both wanted me to tell you that you cause problems in the household when you a woman approach the pastor directly instead of going to the first lady out of respect. Vice versa for the first lady - deacons stop going straight to first lady instead of going to the pastor directly!

The first lady knows you secretly want to sleep with her husband. The pastor knows you trying to break up his home men! So get out of they face and stop being messy.

That is all for now. This announcement has been brought to you on behalf of your pastor and first lady.

Most of y'all see opportunity elsewhere but that loyalty to your community keep you right where you are. You would rather suffer for the rest of your life as long as you suffer with the people you been knowing your entire life lol. That song ...No new friends...has ruined you.

There is HOPE for you. It is not too late to move out of where you been living all your natural born life to seek out opportunity. You can always go back to your hometown once you get established. Find yourself and take a risk. The reward is greater than the unknown.

There was a time when my professional life didn't line up with my personal life. I'm glad to see that it's all starting to come together for the good. All I want is to be at peace! Thank God for the trials and tribulations I survived. I endured so much to be in the current position. Wife, mother of three, growing career, encouraging friend, and most importantly supportive daughter to my parents who have stuck with me through the storms, rain, hurricane, thunder and torpedoes of LIFE.

Probably need to stop going to lunch with those who make the same or less than you AND/OR stop having lunch by yourself sitting in your car being introverted and anti-social. Try going to lunch with the group who makes more than you do. That's why your weekends tend to suck because you do the same thing each week.

Next week, should be your week to take a person out to lunch who makes between $25 - $50 per hour. While at lunch don't talk about other people at work, office shenanigans, or small talk. Try talking about personal growth, dreams, their succession plan, retirement programs, and professional development resources.

First job at the Ouachita National Forest working as a receptionist for the JTPA summer youth program. Mr. Crudup the math teacher taught me how win in the workforce. Learned to shake hands, follow orders, and look people in the eyes.

I was 14 and needed a work permit for this job.

Age 15 - worked at the Arkansas Rehabilitation Center as a janitor and laundry worker. Experienced people looking down on me. Worked hard for little pay but was grateful for my job. Had to walk home or catch the city bus. My classmates would drive by me as I walked home. That's why now I always give my people a ride when I see them walking in uniform.

Age 16 - first real job as a cashier at Price Cutter. Remember crying at the register because the white lady who trained me was really impatient and mean. She wanted me to work faster and count the change back slowly. I worked there off and on until I graduated at 18.

Worked as a cashier for most of my life. Worked at Price Cutter in high school plus college, Walmart for 6 months, and Kroger for 5 years. Walmart works cashiers like slaves. I knew when I experienced picking up that big ass dog food that I wasn't going to be there long.

Working at Kroger taught me the most about life:

First real experience with being called a nigger by a customer. The customer visited the store often. I would cringe every time I saw him. In Conway it was rare to see a happy, black, and fun-loving cashier. My line was always long because my customers only wanted me to check them out. I always had something interesting on my mind to say. I cried at home on my last day there.

Fast forward to my first professional job after graduating from UCA. I was honored to be a secretary in spite of having my bachelor's degree. I figured I had to start somewhere. The supervisor picked me because I spoke Spanish. He felt that if I could translate language then I could easily learn SAS programming language. He was right. After 1.5 years I went from $7 to $15.

I no longer needed to work two jobs. I was making now making enough to retire from Kroger with 5.3 years of service. My goal was to become vested. I did it!

My colleague at the time told me I deserve the promotion but I could tell deep in my heart that she was jealous that our salaries were now similar. She preferred dealing with me as a secretary and not the nationally recognized Survey Coordinator. Ha!

Be that one person in your crew that is ABSOLUTELY fearless when it comes to being a GO-GETTER! You see an opportunity and the next thing you know BOOM BAM POW you are in there like swim-wear.

Everyone else is looking to you for direction, guidance, mentorship, and support when it comes to reaching their dreams, hopes, aspirations, and desires. All you can tell them is DO IT, WORK AT IT, PERFECT YOUR CRAFT, REACH OUT, and TRY YOUR BEST, and when that is not enough TRY IT A DIFFERENT WAY.

Be that bright light in your crew, department, church, school, neighborhood, family, and relationship and get your SHINE on. Don't try to down play the ECLIPSE-like LIGHT that God has given you. Take responsibility in the SHINE and be even more AMAZING. Time to kick it up a notch on this Tuesday evening.

Sing your song with me, "THIS LITTLE LIGHT OF MINE...."

Most coworkers aren't great friends.

After you get liberated from the organization you both worked for then you'll soon see if they were coworkers or great friends. I'm happy to have some great friends who have love for me and reach out as often as possible to share love. This is rare and I don't take their love for granted. They know and understand who they are...THANK YOU for being a great friend! Too many to tag.

Non reciprocating co-workers suck geese eggs.

Sometimes life SUCKS!

It has come to my attention and TODAY I am reminded that life is not fair. Just when you think you are about to get a break in life or in your finances then BAM, POW, BOOM-SHACK-ALACKA then here comes bull crap. It seems as if things are happening one right after the other and I can't get a break. Between taxes, registration, car parts and LABOR, and bills in general - it seems like things are going crazy in my life. I know I am not the only one GOING THROUGH but my story is rare, unique, and has its' purpose.

I know I know I know I know that trouble don't, won't, can't, and SHOULDN'T last always - I am reminded of all those plus the prophetic scriptures. I realize that these trials and tribulations that I am facing are all tests to help bring out who I really am as a person. Some people simply can't take much and wind up in the state hospital because life got the best of them - they had a nervous breakdown and couldn't snap back. Others like me, are ready, willing, and honest about their life challenges. We tend to vent, decompress, write, journal, share, motivate, encourage, reciprocate what we need, and BE AMAZING in spite of our current circumstance. This type of behavior deserves a Nobel Peace Prize or some sort of Olympian medal if you ask me. Life ain't easy and sometimes life SUCKS GEESE eggs but keep it moving.

I try my absolute best to stay positive, surround myself with positive people and positive messages but sometimes I just have to say FUCK THIS SHIT I am tired. I know that I am tired because I am working towards my goals, hopes, dreams, and aspirations in life to become better than my best. It is not easy but someone has to do it - if not me, then who? If not now, then when? TODAY is what I make it and I choose to BE FREE of STRESS. I am laying the burden down as I focus my attention on the things that make me smile and bring me joy. I am GRATEFUL in spite of my life sucking GEESE eggs right now.

Thank you for listening; I just had to get that off my chest real quick. I feel better now lol. Actually I feel EMPOWERED to tackle the day and turn my problems into OPPORTUNITIES for advancing me and my family.

If everyone is eating don't eat.

If everyone is laughing don't laugh.

If everyone is frowning don't frown.

If everyone is leaving don't leave.

If everyone is talking just listen.

If everyone is crying don't cry.

If everyone is driving don't drive.

In life, we tend to do what everyone else is doing to make them feel comfortable. Go against the rules and just be yourself. That's enough. Only you know how you feel. What you are feeling matters the most. Nothing else matters except for how you feel about the situation. By going against the pull of nature, you begin to train your brain to make sacrifices towards a new and improved YOU. This is the key.

Be prepared to feel uncomfortable!

Yesterday I blocked three people from calling and texting my phone. You see, I have learned this year that I can't want it more than they want it for themselves. Best thing to do for my sanity is to literally leave them to their own devices.

An investment in a new phone gave me a feature that I didn't have access to before.

Look at God working things out for me!

If you feel like leaving, LEAVE.

If you feel like learning, LEARN.

If you feel like leading, LEAD.

Truth is that I left my previous job because I felt like I had reached my pinnacle. Everyone kept telling me that supervising the people would be my next level. I know myself and I know my personality is to lead by example and it doesn't take a title to lead the people. I also have recognized the fact that the title supervisor limits the employee's ability to truly connect with their staff on a personal and professional level. I'd rather lead a life of true happiness rather than subject myself to what I see on the daily so I left for greener pastures.

Before I left, I made sure that I had options to choose from. I had learned so much about people, leaders and what was needed for my next level. After earning my Master's degree, I knew that God had called me to be about the solution rather than spending hours discussing why Arkansas is at the bottom of the barrel when it comes to health rankings. Learning is the key to leading.

Someone has to lead, why it can't be YOU!

They'll respect you more after you leave. They'll learn more about how awesome you truly are after you leave. This is how great leaders are remembered. You have a special way of leading the people. Continue to take charge of your life and watch the situation change for the better.

LEAVE, LEARN, and LEAD!

16 Success Her Way

She wouldn't let their fears be projected onto her vision of success. Growth came as she learned to function with a very small inner circle of fearless visionaries.

Walked to the park with the kids while there walked the track once and slid down the kid slide. I'm thinking I had more fun than the kids lol...

Had to top it off with a pretend birthday party at Taco Bell and Sonic's. CJ had to have his favorite mozzarella cheese sticks and Khalia got her favorite bean burrito and Calaysia had her favorite corn dog. Yay! Two tacos were left over for dad...lol

Do something fun today...AND remember Tonya loves you!

When you are doing something, new, amazing, extraordinary, impactful, inspirational, cutting-edge, life-altering, uncommon, adventurous, innovative, creative, and just plain bold then AVERAGE and BELOW-AVERAGE minded people are going to be freely marketing your mission. Let them talk and get used to them talking.

It was Frank Friday. She listened with wise ears. In order to learn, she needed to listen more than she spoke. As she listened, she was compelled to say something. You see, before she opened her mouth she had gathered the data, research, facts and several wise stories. Her acronym speech was ready for the very limited few to hear. What she had to say would be worth more than all the Sunday sermons together. She spoke truth, reality, wisdom, and made news that Frank Friday. Her ears were becoming more powerful than her tongue. She listened....

She used her time wisely. Most of her sisters and brothers didn't realize that a great deal of her time was spent feeding her mind. You see feeding her mind was like bathing, it had to be done once a day to be effective. To feed her mind, she listened well. Listening by audio to Jim Rohn, Zig Zigglar, Les Brown, Tony Robbins, and Lisa Nichols as well as her newfound favorites Nino Brown and Love Dorsey. These listening parties she held alone. Just her, her notepad and ears desiring life wisdom. Her peers wondered how she stayed motivated in the midst of uncertainty and pure chaos. She told simply told them this, if you can't hang around eagles daily then try listening parties. They called her..."Encourager" because she shared valuable insight for living well.

Three skills every person needs. Integrity, Intelligence and Innovation. Without integrity the other two don't matter.

They want the success but aren't willing to go through the struggle you have gone through. Keep working towards getting yourself established and learn to drown out their nonsense. It is merely noise! Keep Pushing Higher

And one last thing...

The folks that write share of inspiration, encouragement, motivation, and empowerment stuff that to remind their selves not to stop trying to do better. It adds fuel to the fire when they get any of the following feedback like... Amen, PREACH, yaaaaaas, you got this, or I needed this! When that feedback is shared... Wew that's the ultimate jet fuel. All smiles to those who inspire, motivate, captivate, educate, and empower others!

When folks think you successful they automatically think you have money for them to borrow or have. Looks can be deceiving. Successful people are trying to make it too. Hell they got bills probably BIGGER bills than you and your lil monthly cell phone bill you crying about.

Try crying about student loans, mortgage, and a car note plus insurance. Let alone taking care of yourself and a family. Success takes sacrifice.

If you are weird, awkward, old-fashioned, crazy, and not what is considered normal then you are absolutely WINNING. True stand outs are just their plan ol self. Be true to who you are. God made you that way.

Okay so I am just realizing that in the private sector that a Master's degree is good but doesn't really mean anything. What is valued is integrity, resourcefulness, productivity and experience!

Focus on celebrating yourself then other folks will hop on your band wagon. Before long y'all will be celebrating all together VICTORY. Birds of a feather_____/.

Time to get those negotiation skills on point. When they hit you with the we'd like for you to move into such and such position. Instead of being emotional let's work towards being strategic about your added value to the team.

So happy right now. In 2016, I had an idea to convene a small group of women and work towards uplifting them one by one. We met for nearly six months straight each Friday on the phone. We talked about so many topics anything and everything. Today I am reminded of why I started those calls. I started those calls to uplift the women who God placed in my circle. So many of the women and men who joined in, spoke up, participated, invited others, and most of all listened in are now on their own paths towards greatness. I used to think that those calls didn't really do anything but now I see they were instrumental to so many of us. It showed me that a little idea can become more than you know with just a little bit of action.

Thank you to any and everyone who supported my Uplift The Woman idea to action. We are all on our path towards GREATNESS~!

Slow down today and nurture your relationship with the secretary, janitor, valet and security guard. Just to put you up on game, these folks are the true gatekeepers of the agency you work for. To honor them simply stop in your frantic rush to your desk and ask them how is their day going so far. Be genuinely interested by working on your body language. They read people well. They know if you just want to hear the usual... Everything is going great... OR...if you really are interested in their day.

I have been in both a secretary and janitor position so I see how folks looked down on me. Over the years I've met some of the most amazing and down to earth people in these professions who are just like me. To be honest, their titles make people overlook who they really are. Most of them are simply retired from a long career in an amazing field, in school, others have had life circumstances to happen, and most are using that job as additional income to fund their dream.

All I'm saying is take time out to get to know a great group of people. They all have the power to make your life a living heaven or hell.

Piss any one of them off and see what happens next. You'll have headaches that you can't figure out why...paycheck late? Trash running over? Missing mail? Boot or ticket on your car? Bad reputation?

Honor the gatekeepers and you can't go wrong!

Can't call yourself a leader if you are only helping yourself and no one is following your lead.

If the people in your inner-circle aren't benefiting from your leadership then you aren't leading them.

True leaders assist, add value, provide resources, connect like-minded people, mentor, guide, redirect, role-model, and inspire others to lead in their own way.

That is an effective-leader in my book~! Please remove leader from your resume, CV, and cover letter if you are only in it for yourself.

There are some people who only are around you to get clues for their next move. They aren't there to compliment or reciprocate what you give out. Instead they are there only to slow down your progress towards your dreams, hopes, desires, and goals. Asking you 1,000 questions plus some about why you do the things you do. When are you going to wake up and see that these people aren't the people who you need around you for this next BIG MOVE? They keep feeding you what you liked but can't, won't and don't feed you what you need to GROW. Because you lack self-esteem and self-confidence you keep them around while they steady bring you nothing but stress, anger, and remind you daily of your past life and who you used to be.

If you really begin to think more highly about yourself and all that you have going on then you will soon realize that they are not ADDING but only SUBTRACTING from what you have. Your next big move will cause you to have to leave, let go, and move away from the very people who say they love you. They love you but not the way you need them to love you. It is not in their heart, soul, mind to help you to grow. You see, your growth would mean their DEATH. They feed off of your inspiration, motivation, empowerment, and encouraging words but lack the knowledge, skill, ability or know-how to GIVE at a level that recognizes their very own growth. It is not in them to GIVE at the level that you GIVE so why do you stay in the pits of their hell when you can decide to be alone to focus on respect for yourself. Get from around them because they are serving absolutely no purpose in your life.

Keep them folks around and you will be twice your age with their mess.

Drops mic.

It is not that my life is perfect because I still have some struggles. But for me, it is all about focusing on the stuff that makes me smile, feel happy, and most importantly celebrating with the people who make me feel like I can do whatever I put my mind to.

I really don't care but I truly hope none of you get it twisted and ever think that I am on social media bragging about my life. I am not bragging but instead sharing my wisdom, life experience, and some of my life struggles (with a bit of cursing lol) to remind YOU that you MATTER and your feelings MATTER TOO.

We are rare dreamers and can't stand to be around mood killers. Killing our smile, joy, peace, and overall happy about life attitude. In spite of the trials and tribulations in our life, we are grateful because a lot of folks didn't make it out but we did. Our favor is what keeps us curiously searching for more out of life.

Get back up rare dreamer! Saddle up on your pony to destination SUCCESS. This next destination will feel like heaven on earth. Be in expectation at all times and you'll start to notice everything lining up.

You set the tone and mood in your environment because you have a HIGH INTERNAL LOCUS OF CONTROL.

I was born in July so please don't make the LEO in me come out. I am trying my absolutely best to make this year count for something. I don't have time for bull crap.

If you are not talking about $$$ and productivity then please don't call, voicemail or text my phone asking me silly questions like, "Tonya, what you up to?"

This question makes my blood boil because you know already that I have several responsibilities that I try my best to attend to. I don't have time to BABYSIT your grown ASS.

I feel better now that I have gotten that off my chest. Some folks need to find something to do and get a damn life. On my phone worried about what I am doing when you should be so freaking busy working on your life dreams that you aren't thinking of my hourly moves. Stop the madness people and focus on your business not someone else's. That is the problem I see.

While you worried about them; you could have checked three things off your TO DO list. Matter of fact. Make a NOT TO DO LIST. #1 should be DO NOT WORRY ABOUT OTHER PEOPLE because THEIR LIFE HAS NOTHING TO DO WITH MINE. Write that down and THANK ME LATER!

Great morning,

Waking up setting goals for my day is the best feeling in the world. Stretch your body and feel free to do your age number in sit ups. We got this!

Drinking water for breakfast to get our system going to regulate the iron pill if you need to be taking one too.

Love yourself more than you love others today.

outburst: a sudden release of strong emotion.

Good for your soul!

———————

FLAT LINE

---------------------------------->

PROGRESS

<---------------------------------

BACKWARDS

The choice is yours to be stagnant,

progressive, or backwards.

Shoutout to all those who are choosing

PROGRESS this week!

As I chase the vision, it seems that the resources continue to pour in. I'm thinking by this time next year there is no telling where me and YOU will be. The more we have the more successful we are. It is all merely a mindset as we train our brain to see the opportunity in every problem. For years, I tried it the wrong way and I'm looking forward to the next 39 chapters of my life being impactful, visionary, and full of stories to share to heal the world around me. This is the key to liberation and total freedom.

The I don't give a FUCK attitude about your personal and professional life will have you where you want, desire, aspire, and need to be in no time! Try it today and thank me later!

Two things that made me happy today. Hugging my mom and dad. Seeing the kids enjoy their grandparents.

It's the little things that matter the most y'all.

What's the biggest risk you took this year?

For me, it was leaving my public health job and starting a career in a totally different field in health care information technology. For me, it was a now or never mindset. It was more about the opportunity than the security. I'm now celebrating 6 months in and the opportunities are still pouring in on a daily basis.

Yes, there were times when I had doubt. I quickly focused my thoughts on why I left in the first place. This has been the key to reminding myself that the risk has been worth it all.

Left a good job for a great life in business and a career within a sector that has system level influence!

What's the longest drive you've taken this year?

I drove 17+ hours non-stop to Cheyenne, Wyoming. Took my family so that they could witness the drive and my DRIVE. Met and connected more with two amazing women while there. So glad that we made it safely there and back. We had some good family bonding. Great memories were made.

Nothing like having family members around as you make career and business moves.

Best feeling in the world is not only doing great work with great people but sharing on a meaningful level that makes life struggles easier to manage. WIN-WIN!

Money is not the root to all evil. It's the person not the paper. That's the root. Consider this a new way of thinking on today as we get the money so that we can change our circumstances. Money empowers intentional minded people to take action on the vision.

Without a community vision then money leads to debt, scarcity, and evil instead of wealth, abundance, and Good Living.

17 The Wise One

The man stopped asking for fish. He finally understood that wisdom came by asking for fishing poles. With fishing poles in hand he cast out and the harvest was plentiful. His family grew because of his wisdom.

The wise men came together to discuss kingdom building. Small talk was not in their nature. Their ideas were solely about sharing wisdom and willpower. They wanted nothing more than to see their kinship grow towards excellence. The village was fruitful and multiplied...

He said what needed to be said. For his fearless ways God rewarded him with the title of truth teller. He was young but sat amongst the elders. The elders looked towards his youth for renewed faith. They called him Truth Teller.

And one more thing before I get my Saturday going! Thank God for my momma and daddy still teaching me at age 39. The other day my mom and I had a discussion about THE BOAT of LIFE!

I love speeches so here it goes in written form:

You are on a boat. On your boat you have two paddles to get to where you need to go. As you are paddling, you notice someone coming close to your boat. At that point you must ask yourself should I keep going or stop to see what the heck they want. You being you all curious and stuff decide to stop. The other person asks for help because their boat is leaking. You quickly tell them to hop aboard. Oh Lord that Jesus helping spirit has got you in a situation. So back to the story...your boatmate asks you where you were headed. You being the happy go lucky person you are tell everything you had planned for the day lol. Stop. Wait. Holdup. YOU should be asking your boatmate where in the hell they going. You don't ask because you got the God-complex trying to help the needy all the time. So...hours go by when you realize you doing all the paddling, boat mate ain't doing shit but relaxing, you start taking notice that boatmate has secretly been carving wholes in your boat. The water starts to come into your boat so you must decide to stay on your boat or abandon your boat. What you do next decides your ability to be resilient when on the BOAT of LIFE!

Moral: Use your Spidey senses when dealing with people on the B.O.A.T. of LIFE!

What I wish I knew then that I know now:

1. With no goals, you'll be helping others reach theirs.

2. The Healthcare Information Technology world is a growing industry with lots of career opportunities for public health minded folks.

3. You get what you give.

4. Delegate

6. Be resourceful and your $$$ will increase.

7. Show yourself integrity.

8. Learn to eat alone in season and out.

9. Accept what you see and know.

10. Get it off your chest you'll feel a hell of a lot better!

The key to good living is to nurture the relationships that make you feel like you floating on cloud 9. Everybody else can go kick rocks.

We are rare so it behooves us to study rarity. Like big diamonds, the eclipse, full moon on a Friday 13th, aligned quasars, rain and sun-shine, and the last fall leaf in the tree YOU are a very RARE sight.

Take ownership of who you are and what is inside of you will become a blessing to the world.

I have heard people say...LaTonya go to school and get you a good education because KNOWLEDGE IS POWER. I am here to tell you today that I have been lied to all these years. Knowledge is only power if and when you use it wisely. I know so many smart, intelligent, degreed, and scholarly people who are sad-mad, depressed, and downright angry because they are in debt up to their eyeballs and their education has not worked in their favor. I see it and hear it all the time. Most folks think that just because you have a high school diploma, bachelors, masters, or even a doctorate that once you graduate that every door of opportunity is going to be open for you to walk in. That is not true because from what I have seen most folks graduate with little to no experience or they don't have a brand or niche in the field or industry they are working in so they are left with only knowledge looking for power.

The key to earning an education is this...you must learn how to apply what you know to an industry that has an opportunity that just right for you. For example, I have worked in the public health industry for nearly 13 years and now I am in the field of Health Information Technology. Two totally different fields of work. Over the years, I have come to understand how to market my niche expertise in writing, skills in communication, abilities in leadership, experience in translating information, and educational background in health education and public health. This has all worked in my favor and I understand that it is not only what I know (KNOWLEDGE) but a combination of it plus APPLICATION of what I know to solve problems.

Yes, get all the degrees, certifications, and trainings possible but also think through where the field or industry is growing and make a mark in the industry. You will soon become the go-to person based on your expertise and your AMAZING ability to apply what you know and break it down into the most simplistic way so that everyone is on the same page. Leaving no one lost when it comes to dealing with the complex issues that we all deal with on a daily basis.

Learn to apply what you have learned before going out to get another degree that you really don't need.

Thank me later for saving you $$$!

Knowledge is power once applied.

Some folks on social media are low key hating on you...

They know who they are and won't for the life of them throw a like, comment, or share on your VERY magical posts that have pure substance. You see their green chat box light on at all times of the day and night but they won't message you and say "You Inspire Me Tonya". They are watching your page for clues about your life and your next move. You keep them confused by posting inspirational, motivational, empowering, and encouraging messages which keep them sad-mad or down right angry.

Like I always say...people are either jealous or inspired but it takes a heck of alot to inspire people who won't set goals for their life. With no goals, their soul brews, spews, and spits hatred, negativity, and their blood pressure stays at 220/989! That bottom blood pressure number is the most important and theirs is steady rising!

Stroke level blood pressure because they won't ask for clues to how to get their life on track. They can stay mad if they want to.

Please don't ever consider deleting them because they are on your "RUN AND GO TELL IT" committee. They do all of your business marketing for free. Your services don't have to be in the newspaper and you don't have to pay for social media ads because they market any and everything you do.

Believe me when I tell you this...watch God use them in your favor to get you on to your next level. Never delete or block the haters because like Sy said - they can be a customer too.

The more you do the more you will realize that you can't make everyone happy! STAY very focused on your GOALS and leave the haters to their job responsibilities.

Leading is similar to pulling a string. First you must slightly pinch the tip of the string. Taking special care to select the top of the string or the bottom. After you choose the direction you want to go then you begin to pull the directionless string along. That's leading...

In this story...

The string = people

The pinch = pain for you and them

Direction = Vision

Top/Bottom = Lion or Sheep

Pull = work to make more leaders

To know the tree, you must take time to understand the root! The root tells the untold story of the tree, it's branches, it's fruit (if any), it's leaves, it's sway, it's type, it's age, and it's sap (if any).

Only on solid foundation can we build.

People that seem to know any and everything seem to come off as intelligent but really and truly they have been through pure hell and back. The experience that they have gained, earned, and battle scared their life with is simply called life wisdom.

At the drop of any conversation, they give the best advice because they have done it all plus MORE. Their ears are so unjudgemental because no one on earth could have actually done anything worse than they have done.

This is the key to being WISE.

Life wisdom comes from living life to the fullest. You can look at other's people life all day and not learn a thing about your life. It's when you start using their example and applying it to fix your credit, get a resume created, take a first time homeowner class, take a class to learn a valuable skill, or simply open your heart up for love again, and that's how positive change begins.

I remember a time when I wanted them to accept me as one of their own. It took years off my life. Now I focus on working towards my own life goals and not theirs. Their will come a day when we all realize that hard work pays off so that we can take those learned skills, talents, knowledge, and abilities to do for self.

No need to be angry with yourself any longer. They see you working like a slave. They know what you could be if they told you your value. Truth is that you will never receive the validation that you are looking for from them. Do for self is simply building your own organization and showing your magnificent idea to those who will appreciate and benefit from it!

There is no wisdom without experience, disappointment, trial, error and failure. If you want life wisdom you must be willing to go through something that others aren't willing to go through.

Leadership requires leaders to initiate. If you don't, then who will do it. You might get tired of going first but just remember that others are taking notice of how to initiate in their own way.

You are making a much needed difference. Always remember that and you'll go further faster. You set your pace and no one else can.

To gain wisdom and insight on next steps for your situation, please look within. Discover your true resilient nature. This test is only going to bring out the best in you.

If it's too much then just simply cry out and say Lord GIVE ME A BREAKTHROUGH! Don't know if I can take it anymore. The burden is as heavy as it can get.

When you are at Rock bottom the only way out is UP!

18 Broken Curses

This is for the one person that needs to forgive their biological father. Holding in that hurt, anger and pain is limiting your full potential. Free yourself today so that you can enjoy the full essence of loving yourself. Do it with a sense of urgency. Let that go!

10 Things To Understand Upfront before you text or message:

No, you will not receive a nude!

No, you cannot borrow my car!

No, you will not loan you $700 to pay your rent!

No, you cannot come over to hang out!

No, you will not get picked up if you get dropped off!

No, you will not get a plate fixed and brought over!

No, you will not get anything off my bank card!

No, you cannot wash my car for $50!

No, you cannot watch the kids for $20 each!

No, No, No!

This is for that one person who is all tore up on the inside because they are listening to the opinion of another person.

Ask yourself, who are they to listen to?

You are a lion and folks with an opinion are sheep.

Consider this ... Lions don't worry about the opinion of a sheep. Lions are powerful and when they roar the jungle takes notice. As a lion, you can not afford to allow the jungle animals to silence your roar. Anyway, what's a sheep baaaaa baaaaa baaaa gone do for a hungry lion (((ROAR ROAR ROAR))). Sheeps get ate the hell up lol.

Everybody has that one person in their family that keeps everyone on edge. Every day it is something different. Makes you want to throw in the towel until you put yourself in their shoes. When your people are stressed out they can't make good decisions. Love them anyway. It's not easy but WWJD!

Marry up not down! They family doing worse than your family. What is that going to do for you and your blood pressure? Long term it's a fatal decision to marry him/her because y'all have good sex.

What about intelligence, go-getter spirit, dreams, goals, and family values?

Keep pushing strong something better awaits you!

I had to risk everything but on the other side of the unknown I didn't imagine a life of reward, flexibility, health, proximity and true freedom.

In life, we have two choices GROWTH or DECAY. Most of y'all decaying and are extremely mad about it. Stay mad. People try to help you but you don't want help thinking you know everything plus some.

Sit down and be humble to GROW. My mentors teach me what they wish they knew at my age. Find someone to mentor you or stay mad.

Truth is...you are too proud to ask LaTonya Bynum for clues. You don't want me to know you decaying but the truth is I already see it. You just need to come clean and ask for GROWTH assistance.

Love talking to my mother with my dad in the background hollering "Hey TonkePooh". This morning, my mother and I had an interesting conversation. I am always trying to describe to her what I do in my new line of work in Healthcare IT.

To the young girl contemplating giving up her virginity this weekend. Don't do it. If he really likes you he'll wait. Plus if you make him wait he'll respect you a lot more than the other girls who will simply give in. Don't worry yourself too much about what he thinks, feels, and needs from you. Yes, he makes you feel special right now but after it is all said and done you'll be upset with yourself. If he loves you, he'll respect you enough to see that you are worth waiting for. Boys want sex and a man wants you to be fully ready. Big difference.

You are special enough to wait for.

While visiting my parents this weekend, I took the kids by to see the land I bought for them. I have three lots and three kids. So I was like you get a lot CJ, you get a lot Khalia, and you get a lot Calaysia.

Before they were born, I paid less than $1,000 for all three of them. Ask me how the Arkansas Land Commission is basically gifting land to generate local and state tax revenue. People don't pay their taxes and so the land commission auctions off land and properties for a little of nothing. You buy them with a limited warranty deed and hold for a couple of years them bam if the owner don't pay it's yours after you secure a full warranty deed.

Instead of worrying about material stuff and bogus activities I pay the taxes on their LAND. They won't have to worry about being in this world without a spot to call their own.

I'm not bragging just trying to inspire another parent to think BIG when it comes to giving your kids material stuff vs. assets that will lessen their burden as they build their own version of multi-family generational wealth.

Love talking to my mother with my dad in the background hollering "Hey TonkePooh". This morning, my mother and I had an interesting conversation. I am always trying to describe to her what I do in my new line of work in Healthcare IT.

Recently at work, one of our system servers shut completely down. The root cause of the problem was linked back to too many connections. This is profound.

Sometimes in life you will experience no connections, limited connections, and way too many connections. When you have way too many connections it tends to be overwhelming especially if the connections are taxing your system resources (i.e. your mental and physical health).

I have found myself in a position where I had way too many connections and I simply did like the system. I shut down. It is okay to shut down but during the rebooting process assess the connections before re-establishing a direct link. May need to MONITOR and rethink each and every connection then set up some guidelines, protocols, processes, and procedures to prevent another system SHUT DOWN.

Moral to the story: Choose your connections wisely.

Mental abuse is the worst kind of torture because it doesn't leave scars on your body instead leaves scars on your mind. All scars take time to heal.

Had a talk this morning with a coworker about family. Family will always be the same. You can talk to them until you are black and blue in the face but you still going to realize that they will do what they want. It is going to take more than you to make them do what is right with their life. Instead of wasting your time on them decide today to focus on yourself.

Be in the moment today with what your dreams, goals, hopes and aspirations is for life. Chances are you will be twice your age if you wait on them to follow your instructions and lead them into their destiny.

I have found that over time - family can do a number on your mental strength and fortitude. You see, they know you best. They have been around you most of your life. They know what makes you happy, sad, tired, and definitely know what makes you tick. There aren't many people who have been around you to study you like a book. Once you realize that they know you best and understand that you have a very limited view of what your purpose then you will be a whole lot better off. You see, they understand and have seen your past failures, ups, and successes in life so they can easily hold that stuff against you or use it to inspire you to become better than your best.

It is rare for a family member to be the essence of positive energy and use that energy to continually to wake you up out of your deep sleep. If you have a family member who brings pure messiness, unhappiness, depression, and a lack of direction to your life then this POST is for you. Because you don't see any value in what you bring to the table, they play mind games on you. They keep you thinking that you need them when in all actuality it is the other way around. They need you to survive. You can't thrive until you let go of them. Family will be okay when and if you decide to do your own thing. Just think of it like this...someone has to go off and be GREAT because living every day like this means no one is ever going to become better than their best.

Sit around talking and complaining about what. For what. How is that helping anything? Not once have they had an original unique idea that benefits both of you. You have low self-esteem and low self-confidence and they continue to feed into it each and every day of your life. You wonder why when someone compliments you then you immediately get mad. It is because you have become the essence of the spirit loosed by your family member.

You are most like the people who are around and talk to.

Get away as far away as possible from them. They will be the same people as they are today if you don't change first. Be the beacon of light for your family. Show yourself that you bring light. Don't get me wrong it is lonely but it will definitely get better as you learn to love yourself. Your relationships will benefit once you drop the negativity you are surrounded by. You deserve to be happier than you have ever been. YOU MATTER.

Black people need government system navigators to WIN. Navigators are community leaders who can translate what the hell is going wrong in our community. No sugar coating but straight facts with documented evidence coupled with resources to do better.

Other races observe and research black problems and make millions off of our community lack of direction and self-worth!

No more silent suffering...

One day soon every corner of my household will be used for business operations.

Blocked by my first #cousin!

Recently I noticed one of my first cousins blocked me. I was sorry to find this out - it was on my mind a lot lately because I love and care for my family. I was listening to one of my #motivational videos today and it gave me some great #insight on this situation between the two of us.

You see, she blocked me because my life, posts, and force of good in the world is a constant reminder that we grew up together having the same #opportunities for advancement but she decided NOT to push herself as hard as she could. To be honest, she has always been a straight A student - actually taught me long division. She has made some choices in life that have led her to where she is now - pain, dysfunction, full of excuses and drama. I continually experience failure, resilience, and breakthroughs in every part of my life. She has the ability to use her intelligence and healing nature to do GREAT things in the world. It is never too late. Until she sees it for herself, she'll forever remain in that dark shadow that she lives in. No one could bring me to this light I see. I had to open up my eyes and truly want more LIGHT for myself.

I understand NOW that my light shines into the dark places of her life so blocking me is the best option until she can see herself as the person I know she is and who she was made to be for the man above. Lord knows I love her so but I must do what is best for me and my immediate family. All this good positive energy is not what she wants right now. I have the responsibility to walk in peace.

We grew up together but NOW I realize...she ONLY wants to remember who I was as a kid under her light but can't stomach the WOMAN I am becoming - a powerful force of nature walking in God's light.

Cain killed able!

Some of us will get taken out or thrown out of focus because of our love for family. That's what is killing your vibe - not your coworkers, neighbors or random folks you meet on a daily basis.

No, it's the people who have studied you and observed your smiles and sadness. They are the ones who have the ability to take you out.

Once you realize this your life will instantly become better! The bible scriptures can be applied to current day in time stuff we are facing. Read it and apply it. Cain killed Able!

As I get older and raise my kids, I have a real appreciation for my mom and dad. What it takes to raise and care for a family is courage, Patience, and a heart filled with love. Not easy but we must constantly remind ourselves of where we came from. Building on the great training and leadership we have experienced so that our kids and their kids may have a better quality of life. My mom and dad did a great job raising me their best so that I could hit the ball out of the park for mine! Getting better by the day with not one, not two, but three little leaders in training. Hugging them and kissing them constantly as they grow up before my eyes...

A lot of us don't realize how truly valuable we are in our field. This message is for that one person who is reading this who is giving away free advice, support, encouragement, empowerment, and coaching tips but your bank account is not looking any different. Start asking yourself what are these folks coming to me for and what is my hourly rate...

This will make all the difference in your world. There is nothing wrong with getting paid for the value you bring to the table. We have never been taught how to think like a businessman/woman.

Let them go you'll be better off in the long run. I promise you'll miss their good side but every hour of dealing with their bad side takes 1 year off your life. Loneliness is a good thing when it comes to peace of mind! Your life is valuable. Always remember that first and foremost.

You only get one life. Live your life to the MF fullest extent possible by law. Time waits for no one!

19 Creative Genius

Study common sense, elderly wisdom, effective communication, and human behavior... those are the keys to a great start at life. Develop skills to do it casually and on purpose.

Don't take that career mess into your beautiful weekend filled with friends, family and fun. Those folks at work are helping you to become better than your best. After all 5 years from now, what you worried and having a pity party about is not going to matter anyway. Chances are you won't remember the story you keep replaying over and over in your mind.

Analyze your self-worth and value to those who matter the most. Don't spend your entire weekend moody about what happened or what is happening at work. Use the weekend to apply for a new job where you can be celebrated and not be miserable.

They wouldn't understand even if you spent two hours and twenty five minutes trying to explain it to them. Might as well just show them through action how it's done. This works better than spending your energy about to lose your voice trying to reason with them.

They can't relate to you and why you do the things you do.

Former Drug dealers make some of the best supervisors and business professionals. They know what people want and what people need. I learned from them that the WORKPLACE is really all about the ability to HUSTLE and transfer PEOPLE-SKILLS.

Yesterday, I played a game on social media that asked some of you to tag your name in the comment section and I would describe you in four words. This morning, I woke up thinking about the gift God has blessed me with. He places special words in my heart to either say or write. That is a precious gift. I reviewed what I wrote yesterday and realized that I didn't use the same word more than once. Each time I thought of the person and how they made me feel and that's the word that came to my mind. How many times have we felt good about someone but haven't, wouldn't, couldn't, or just plain old don't put it out there and tell them how you truly feel. Life is short you better get that off your chest today. If it helps just channel your inner LaTonya Bynum power and simply say what comes to mind no filter! Thank me later...

They want your success but ain't willing to put in the work. You make it look easy. Hard work + Resilience = Your Legacy

It is never too late to try to become better than what you think is your best. There is more to life than your current perspective.

Might be time to flip the game around on them. Put yourself in the position to where you are the calling the shots. Hell you are already in a powerful position to make some serious money moves. The only thing about it is that you have been around so many people who feed into your low self-esteem, self-doubt, insecurity, and light-dimming behavior.

BUT TODAY, you are AWAKE and realize you want to do BETTER than your BEST. Time to shake up some things while letting absolutely no one - I mean - NOT ONE PERSON in your circle know what you are about to do next...trust no one not even your momma for this next MOVE. They will see it later anyway so why tell them now!

I don't work I make $ money $ moves - LaTonya B.

White supremacy makes me work harder NOT give up easier. Black Girl Magic MOVES all this week.

Our children are the future. Train them up to believe they a LEADERS and they will LEAD us into the FUTURE. Remind them daily that they can be anything they put their mind to.

What is Black Girl Magic?

It is when you walk into the room and you immediately change the energy from mediocre to excellent. It is having the wisdom of a woman twice your age. It is listening more than you talk so that you elders both spiritual and actually present can speak to you. It is being the best at what is required of you. It is providing resources, information, and insight to people on a level that only they can understand. It is being a great mother, wife, and daughter all at once because you know someone is always watching. It is about being a trendsetter in your group. It is finding time to do the things that bring you joy, peace, and utter happiness so that you can fight the good fight. It is focusing on self-care because you see women twice your age trying to heal *from years of suffering in silence. It is having degrees, certifications, and scholarly accolades that most can only imagine. It is being a great cousin, friend, and sister to those who need you the most. It is being the real, true, authentic person who God made you. Plus on top of that, speaking the truth to empower others to come out of their own darkness into a light that will illuminate a path for more Black Girl Magic.*

Talking about shit that don't matter is an absolute waste of time. I still remember carrying on pointless conversations when I didn't have the confidence to really and truly say what's on my mind. Now I'll quickly say what's going on. What's on your mind. This is the same as saying...you are not going to waste my time beating around the bush. Let's get straight to the point. After giving my best advice, I'll quickly end the conversation with a written contract and request their John Hancock signature. I realize that some folks truly need direction and something to work towards. So I give them what they need instead of what they thought they were going to get: time wasted. When they see or think of you, they'll think of that contract vs. wasting time in another pointless conversation about nothing.

Don't allow people to waste your precious time. Time is all we have to work on our dreams, goals, and life aspirations.

Most of us don't realize that being nosey is the same thing as being a great researcher. Just think about it. You can go to people social media pages and find out things about them by reading, looking at their mutual friends list, and investigating their photos, etc. I have done it myself so I know it is true. I can generally find out anything I want to know based on a couple of key research skills that I have learned over the years. The key to quality research is to look up some stuff that is going to improve your life.

The library is wide open, the internet stays open 24/7, and your phone is a great device for looking up some stuff. I don't know why some of us sit up and worry about all the wrong things when we have technology available and ready for us to learn, do, and see almost anything our heart desires. Be nosey and make your life better and stop worrying about all the wrong stuff.

I always say to myself...If it don't make $$$ it don't make sense.

Nosey=Great Researcher

P.S. Research skills are very valuable in certain industries. They are called subject matter experts in the HIT field that I work in.

I got 99 problems but MENTORING ain't one...

Shout out to all my mentees/mentors who understand the art and science of reverse mentoring...

On any given day, I become the mentee and you become the mentor. Vice versa with me sharing my insight...

We never drain each other because it's constant pouring from you and pouring from me...

This is the key to RECIPROCAL mentorships!

No need to tag you because you know who you are...we are OFFICIAL mentor and mentee!

Today I developed job listing resource document and shared it on LinkedIn, Gmail, and Facebook. I received lots of interest in the document. One lady gave me some pointers on what to do to perfect it to help even more people who work in the healthcare and public health industries. Basically, she asked me to tell her more about how to apply and tailor her public health skills to market her skills, talents, and abilities to Fortune 500 companies.

I have some ideas on how to help her and others like her. So many ideas.

Next up, I plan to come up with a resource document for people with a high school education or less looking for jobs in the AR area. I have some ideas on how to improve public health - starting with a decent job that pays well.

So much to do to assist my people...this is the type of stuff that keeps me thinking about URA Resource Center, LLC

Try not to spend your time explaining your value to people who are not interested in your growth.

That time can be spent getting ready to go where they will never be able to go. Believe me when I tell you that somethings are truly unexplainable to people.

20 No Excuses

Life Lessons based on 39 years of life in the rural South of Arkansas, USA

#1 Your family has the first shot at taking you out or helping you to grow. Figure out who is who!

#2 Nice people finish last. Be naughty nice

#3 Every friend is there for a season or a reason. Enjoy the 4 seasons you have!

#4 People pleasing is a spirit. Let it go and focus on your gut feeling!

#5 Never meet a stranger!

#6 Married folks lie to make married life look appealing. It's hard work. Be ready to work at it daily.

#7 Do You! Don't worry about how others are going to feel. Those who love you are happy if you are happy!

#8 Only time you going to hear how they truly feel is when you die to live!

#9 Racism and all the other isms were here before me and will be here after me. So break through barriers anyway.

#10 Without mental fortitude, you will be in the Arkansas State Hospital. Tapped the hell out.

#11 Find love and cherish the hell out of it. It alone will give you strength.

#12 Coochie cobwebbs make women angry. They just need a fat one to cool them off. Anger is internal.

#13 Realize that your family members are studying your every move – they will be the most lethal weapon in taking you clear out and off track.

#14 Enjoy the present. It is a present!

#15 Be careful of allowing older men to lick on your private parts. They tend to use that as a technique to play mind games and control your every move

#16 Everybody shit stank. I mean everybody. Let that soak in.

#17 Education starts by learning to read people then moves you to start reading books to research what you see as truth.

#18 Most folks only have a career but are too busy to start a life. What's the purpose of prosperity with no one to share it with.

#19 Friends will let you down but God will not. Look within yourself for true friendship. Friends are in the SHIT HOUSE!

#20 All that black power studying is only useful if applied. Just like bible scripture. Application leads to results.

#21 Folks use you only if you want them too.

#22 Healthy parents are a blessing.

#23 If it don't feel right then run like hell.

#24 Some white folks will treat you better than your own people. Just say thank you for lending their privilege. Don't blow it out of proportion.

#25 Black folks will heal when we see the need. The healing starts within yourself!

#26 Hypertension is environmental. Who is stressing you the hell out? Get them away from you.

#27 A good woman will go the extra mile when she sees potential.

#28 Acronyms help the voiceless find their true voice.

#29 Suck it.

#30 Say what you feel and don't look back. You only wrong if you change your mind later.

#31 Single women cry at night. Praying for their pastor to release them from servitude. Free yourself.

#32 Obesity is silent suicide.

#33 Ask for assistance not help.

#34 I'm not responsible or dependable.

#35 Self-care is not selfish. The "S" on my chest is not for super anything!

#36 Tell the absolute unadulterated truth even if you are scared

#37 Set boundaries and enforce them as if your life depends on it for survival

#38 Find your happiness and work at re-defining what is needed for joy

#39 Reciprocate with your 3 emergency contacts and find unique ways to support their vision and mission for life

Bonus: Write to stop the overthinking process that hinders most straight A & B students

It is never too late to try to become better than what you think is your best. There is more to life than your current perspective.

Might be time to flip the game around on them. Put yourself in the position to where you are the calling the shots. Hell you are already in a powerful position to make some serious money moves. The only thing about it is that you have been around so many people who feed into your low self-esteem, self-doubt, insecurity, and light-dimming behavior.

BUT TODAY, you are AWAKE and realize you want to do BETTER than your BEST. Time to shake up some things while letting absolutely no one - I mean - NOT ONE PERSON in your circle know what you are about to do next...trust no one not even your momma for this next MOVE. They will see it later anyway so why tell them now!

I don't work I make $ money $ moves - LaTonya B.

Don't be the one that allows your past get into the way of your FUTURE.

Success is a lonely place. Get used to being to yourself. Get used to listening to your inner voice. Your past will have you feeling like an imposter. That's just noise. The enemy within is the only enemy that can do harm. Train your mind, thoughts, and meditate to slow down that rat race in your head. Being calm in the midst of these next few storms, trials and tribulations will help you go where others can't imagine going. Get used to loving YOU now. Thank me later.

Everybody in crisis. Either you just came out of one, you going into one soon, or you in one now. Best thing to do is to not give up on yourself. After all, you have had the victory in much worse situations. The stuff you going through right now is simply NOISE to throw you off track.

Telling folks your dreams is for the birds. When you feel like death is setting in on your body, mind, and soul then realize what is happening before it is too late. Waiting around for your employer, coworkers, family and friends to give you the insight, clues, and wisdom that you need is like waiting for another eclipse. You will be waiting for a long time before you witness someone coming to you with what you need to live a better life. Telling them your hopes, dreams, and inspiration is only going to slow you down in the long run. Truth is you lack the self-confidence and appreciation for your vision plus you don't believe God blessed you with such an original idea. Instead of going out and making the dream become a reality you sit around and tell all the people who secretly want to be you or on the low want to take you out so they can live your life. All the encouraging conference, prayers, texts, writings, quotes, and phones calls don't matter whatsoever if you truly don't believe in your talent, skills, and ability. The struggle is so real therefore it is an absolute must to SHUT THE FUCK UP, keep quiet, listen to your inner voice, and move when no one is looking for you to make a move. Keep them guessing about what your plans and where you draw your positive energy. That is the key to good quality living.

These folks don't care about you anyway. Loyal my ass.

Drops mic once again.

For the last couple of weeks, I have been waking up from a deep sleep. You see, I have been sleep in spirit for a mighty long time. Until recently, I did not realize how my Black Girl Magic was working in my favor. Let me just say this right off top. This phenomenon of our magical powers is so real that it is almost unexplainable. Most folks experience failure but don't, won't, can't, and decide not to get back up and try again. I have failed so many times that it is not funny. I can't describe to you how many times that I failed and thought to myself how was I going to go on another day. I realize now that I had to fail in order to succeed in life. You see, every failure meant that I was learning ways to make better decision, make greater sacrifices, and defiantly take time out to use what I learned to grow. So now, at the age I am now people ask me - why do you speak with such passion, why do you feel the need to keep trying when you have so much already, why do you try so hard. I simply tell them this if I think they can comprehend - Why not be all that I can be and work at it daily. I can rest when I die but until I die you will find me continually working in my Black Girl Magic

You can't teach a "Go-Getter" spirit into someone. If they don't have the drive, passion, and know-how that you are looking for it is going to be really hard to get them where you want them to be. Just like in customer service position, some folks just don't have a friendly gene in their bone. They aren't really fit to be upfront dealing with the customers at all. They will leave your business without any cash flow because they run off off all your friendly people plus customers note when they working and don't come in. That Go-Getter spirited person is a great listener, empathizer, and has a steep learning curve. Tell them something then they will complete the task with a little something extra. You are quickly amazed at these type of people because they are absolutely rare in form. This post is for you if you are a GO-GETTER and make things happen on a regular basis. You might be like me and not be a supervisor but you understand how to lead people. Everyone comes to you for advice, feedback and constructive criticism because they trust you. They know that you have seen it all, have wisdom in most situations, and most importantly don't take no shit from nobody. You don't have to be a supervisor to lead the team into the mission. Remember that and you will go far GO-GETTER. On top of that, supervisors deal with so much stress but you have the option to deal with it or not because you enjoy doing above and beyond your job duties. Stay in your lane when you feel the need to but if the spirit moves you to switch into the supervisor lane then lead. You have spiritual discernment about when and where to work your GO-GETTER spirit.

If you are a GO-GETTER or know of a GO-GETTER thank them for their efforts. You might learn something that you can use to make your life better.

Some folks don't want you to dust off your shelf...

They would rather you leave your shelf dusty, leaning over about to fall down, and overall looking a straight mess. Rather than assist you with dusting it off, they would rather you not mention your shelf. You see, mentioning your shelf makes them think about their shelf. The truth is that if you start the process of dusting off your shelf you will make them take a closer look at their shelf. They don't have it in them just yet to focus on their shelf. With you two being on different pages about the importance of shelf cleaning, either you will start cleaning and stop listening to them. OR wait on them to give you permission to clean your shelf. OR wait on them to start thinking about cleaning their shelf. Truth is your people pleasing spirit will have you twice your age waiting on the people you love to make a move. Can't, don't, and won't wait on anyone but YOU. Time to *make a power move as if a PIT BULL is about to bite your heels off. Overthinking this type of stuff will leave you literally ATE up!*

Time to make up your mind today about the importance of your shelf life. By organizing and cleaning your shelf off, you'll begin to feel better. That is all that matters. Your clean shelf will inspire, motivate, encourage, and empower others to stop being in denial about what's on their shelf. If you inspire no one at least your shelf is clean and you feel vibrant and full of life about how you took action and made a huge difference in your life.

Don't worry about their shelf but instead stay focused on cleaning your shelf and making sure to dust it off every now and then after the clean-up happens. Once your shelf is clean and properly established on firm foundation then and only then can you be a bright light for shelf cleaning.

Those same folks you putting on a high pedestal all boo boo on a toilet and flush just like you.

But, not everyone washes their hands singing the happy birthday song. Okay that's a public health joke.

You desire to shake their hands

You desire to be in their circle

You desire to learn their successful ways

You desire to be better than them

Learn to tell your story. Your truth will set you free like the people you want to be.

The key to life is to NEVER compare but just

BE AWARE of what has happened to you.

Big difference to level up in life.

We are not designed to do what we think of as uncomfortable.

You can be the best parent, best spouse, and best at what you want to do. Realize that you are one decision away of being better.

Learn the technique that I use each morning -

5-4-3-2-1! DO IT with no hesitation. NASA!

Spot light effect is something to learn too.

Thank me later because motivation is GARBAGE.

Are you driven?

A lot of us on social media need assistance with our goals. We must not think of ourselves as needing help. To me help has a very negative notion to it. If someone asks me for help, my brain automatically feels overwhelmed at what I have the ability to do to fix their situation. However, if someone asks me for assistance with their situation then I'm thinking...they have been working on it but need me to assist them get the rest of the way. On this note, we must be careful with choosing our words wisely. We all *have gifts and some of us are more talented in certain areas. By asking each other for assistance, we can reach our goals even quicker. I love to write, analyze, and speak then you may love to read, evaluate and listen so we complement each other when we assist with our gift. Hope this helps someone to understand that there is a big difference in asking for "help" and "assistance" as we all learn the art and science of RECIPROCITY!*

I decree and declare that the law of attraction will work extremely in our favor this week. I see and feel miracles like Raises, Promotions, Bonuses, Debt Cancellations, Acing of Assignments, Amazing Health, Loving Relationships Abound from Friends and Family, and Positive Coworkers Showing Out for Team Wins! High Expectations is the new mindset we need to kick things into high gear in the last few days of 2020!!!

As we do things that have never been done, you'll start to feel like you are the only one. God will send you a ram in the bush to remind you that you are not alone.

We must not let our mind play tricks on us.

Tricks are for kids! Do it and they will come!

We are all very powerful people but we just don't know it yet. The day we decide to stop running down the list of people who will approve or disapprove of our decisions will be the same exact day we start to live a powerful life. Solving world problems by solving our own problems. This is the greatest art of all.

About the Author

LaTonya Bynum was born and raised in Hot Springs, Arkansas and earned her college prepatory diploma from the Hot Springs High School. In high school, LaTonya took the discovery assessment which identified her as passionate about helping others. Equipped with the results of the discovery assessment, she applied and was accepted as a student at the University of Central Arkansas in Conway, Arkansas.

She holds a Bachelors of Science in Health Education with a concentration in Community Health and Spanish from the University of Central Arkansas. In addition, she earned her Master's in Public Health (MPH) with an emphasis in Health Policy and Management from the University of Arkansas for Medical Sciences.

As a Technical Editor with DXC Technology, a global IT company, she now has a combined total of over twenty years of experience in Retail Sales, Public Health, and Health Information Technology. This editor position led to her first self-published book titled "Tools for Career Success: 101 FAQs about Public Health" and now the second book titled "Mind Ya Busi-

ness: Are You Okay?". Furthermore, she is humbled to hold the mantle of being the first in her immediate family to earn a bachelor and master's degree.

She has served as a passionately-curious certified health education specialist also known as CHES in several program capacities (i.e. Hospital Discharge Data System, Behavioral Risk Factor Surveillance System, County Adult Health Survey, Synar Surveillance System and the Office of Rural Health and Primary Care) at the Arkansas Department of Health for over 12 years, she was able to develop niche skills in writing, public speaking and research / data analysis that led to her interest in public health consulting for clients and organizational leaders.

LaTonya enjoys analyzing data and conducting research to write scientific papers. Her graduate level MPH work titled "The Role of Depression in Chronic Disease Management: An Analysis of the U.S. Behavioral Risk Factor Surveillance System" is published in the Public Health Open Access Journal. Additionally, she has co-authored papers regarding Falls and Comorbid Conditions, Diabetic Retinopathy, and Eye Care Services.

About URA Resource Center, LLC

In 2017, LaTonya founded U.R.A. Resource Center, LLC, a public health consulting firm with the sole mission to Utilize Research for Access in improving the health status and quality of life of all mankind.

URA Resource Center, LLC is an Arkansas based Woman-Owned and Minority-Owned Federal Government Contracting Small Business with a reputation of providing some of the top public health consultants in the industry. URA Resource Center, LLC has extensive experience conducting Project Management support for creative/technical writing, research, training / meeting facilitation. Support to state regulated facilities who acknowledge the Public Health Accreditation Board standards. URA Resource Center, LLC has developed long term relationships with our clients through our outstanding technical support staff and our commitment to client satisfaction. It is our outstanding technical staff and our unwavering commitment to our clients that sets us apart from other vendors / suppliers

- Serving over four-hundred (400) national and international clients by recommending valuable career resources (i.e. curriculum vitae, resume and cover letters), job search listings and tips, mentorship advice, *job interview preparation and salary offer /negotiation sessions via Zoom, and quality training programs focused on public health standards and evidence-based practices.*

- *Mentors and trains over forty (40) aspiring and currently Certified Health Education Specialist (CHES) clients through the Think Like a Health Educator (TLHE) program. The TLHE CHES exam pass rate is 83% compared to the 63% national NCHEC pass rate.*

- *Provided five (5) business organization contractual consultations for creative and technical writing assistance and consultations for public health event technical assistance / public health worker training, needs assessments, meeting facilitation and programmatic reports.*

- *Developed an active and engaged network of over six-thousand (6,000) community members, students, emerging and seasoned professionals on LinkedIn, Instagram, Twitter, YouTube and Facebook. Popular topics of discussion include personal development, career advancement and business start-up and growth success.*

- *Sub-contracting over twenty (20) paid projects to URA Resource Center, LLC consultants, interns and mentees with special skills in creative and technical writing, public speaking and research/data analysis.*

www.ingramcontent.com/pod-product-compliance
Lightning Source LLC
Chambersburg PA
CBHW022104160426
43198CB00008B/345